Sharing Mobilities

This book examines contemporary urban sharing mobilities, such as shared and public forms of everyday urban mobility. Tracing the social and economic history of sharing mobilities and examining contemporary case studies of mobility sharing services, such as Car2go, BlaBlaCar, and Uber, the authors raise questions about what these changes mean for access to and engagement with the public spaces of transport in the city. Drawing on the thought of Lefebvre, the book considers how contemporary sharing mobilities are affecting people's 'right to the city', with particular attention paid to the privatised, frictionless practices of movement through the city. In addition, the authors ask what has happened to earlier forms of shared mobility and illustrate how some of these practices continue successfully today. Considering the potential that modern incarnations of shared mobilities offer to urban citizens for engaging in meaningful shared mobilities that are not simply determined by the interfaces of technology and market forces, this book will appeal to sociologists and geographers with interests in mobility and urban studies.

Davide Arcidiacono is a researcher in Economic Sociology at the University of Catania, Italy. His research focuses on the issues of digital transformation and the sharing and platform economy.

Mike Duggan is a teaching fellow in the Department of Digital Humanities at King's College London, UK. His research focuses on the intersections between digital technologies and everyday cultures of practice.

Sharing Mobilities
Questioning Our Right to the City in the Collaborative Economy

Davide Arcidiacono and Mike Duggan

FOREWORD BY JULIET B. SCHOR

LONDON AND NEW YORK

First published 2020
by Routledge
2 Park Square, Milton Park, Abingdon, Oxon OX14 4RN

and by Routledge
52 Vanderbilt Avenue, New York, NY 10017

Routledge is an imprint of the Taylor & Francis Group, an informa business

First issued in paperback 2021

© 2020 Davide Arcidiacono and Mike Duggan

The right of Davide Arcidiacono and Mike Duggan to be identified as authors of this work has been asserted by them in accordance with sections 77 and 78 of the Copyright, Designs and Patents Act 1988.

All rights reserved. No part of this book may be reprinted or reproduced or utilised in any form or by any electronic, mechanical, or other means, now known or hereafter invented, including photocopying and recording, or in any information storage or retrieval system, without permission in writing from the publishers.

Trademark notice: Product or corporate names may be trademarks or registered trademarks, and are used only for identification and explanation without intent to infringe.

British Library Cataloguing-in-Publication Data
A catalogue record for this book is available from the British Library

Library of Congress Cataloging-in-Publication Data
Names: Arcidiacono, Davide, author. | Duggan, Mike, author.
Title: Sharing mobilities: questioning our right to the city in the collaborative economy / Davide Arcidiacono and Mike Duggan.
Description: Abingdon, Oxon; New York, NY: Routledge, 2020. | Includes bibliographical references and index.
Identifiers: LCCN 2019033654 (print) | LCCN 2019033655 (ebook) | ISBN 9780367192426 (hardback) | ISBN 9780429201288 (ebook)
Subjects: LCSH: Urban transportation. | Ridesharing. | Cooperation.
Classification: LCC HE305 .A735 2020 (print) | LCC HE305 (ebook) | DDC 388.4—dc23
LC record available at https://lccn.loc.gov/2019033654
LC ebook record available at https://lccn.loc.gov/2019033655

ISBN: 978-0-367-19242-6 (hbk)
ISBN: 978-1-03-208785-6 (pbk)
ISBN: 978-0-429-20128-8 (ebk)

Typeset in Times New Roman
by codeMantra

Contents

List of figures vi
List of tables vii
Foreword by Juliet B. Schor viii
Acknowledgements xi

1 Welcome to the age of sharing 1

2 The successes and failures of shared urban mobility 13

3 Sharing mobility, mobility justice, and the right to the city 40

4 Regulation, platform governance, and the labour practices of shared urban mobility 53

5 Empowering connections: relations, collaborations, and community in sharing mobility 78

6 Conclusion 98

Bibliography 111
Index 129

Figures

2.1	Sharing mobility ecosystem	16
2.2	Types of sharing mobility	17
2.3	Historical evolution of shared mobility	24
2.4	Estimated mobility as a service (MaaS) market capitalisation worldwide from 2025 to 2035 (in billions of US dollars)	26
2.5	Start-ups financed worldwide (%)	27
2.6	Reasons given for subscribing to the Car2go service (multiple choice %)	35
5.1	The characteristics of a sharing mobility community	91

Tables

2.1 Top ten decacorn start-up   27
5.1 The types of social relation mapped onto different sharing mobility services   86

Foreword

As the "sharing economy" enters its second decade, we are in a position to take stock of how things have gone, particularly in relation to the ambitious promises with which it was launched. In the early years (2008–2012), when many sharing companies and organisations were founded, they put forward a discourse of common good. They would increase efficiency, access, and incomes. They would reduce environmental footprints, especially for carbon. They would bring strangers together in relations of mutual trust, thereby fostering social cohesion and engagement. Ten years later, many of these claims are in tatters, as investor imperatives led for-profit companies to prioritise growth over socially positive outcomes. Socially minded entities who are committed to the public welfare have failed to scale like the profit-oriented businesses. Sharing has become an increasingly awkward term to describe entities like Airbnb and Uber, given their outsized commercial ambitions and unanticipated impacts.

To some extent, the common good claims were always suspect. Sharing platforms say that they are engines of economic prosperity, dramatically expanding consumer markets, and providing increased incomes for providers. But when they are successful in expanding production, they surely increase climate emissions, as we have not yet reached a stage of de-carbonisation in which more economic activity can occur without a bigger footprint. As lodging platforms expanded, and absent hosts proliferated, desire and opportunity for social connection disappeared. Guests just wanted a better lodging value or a different experience than a hotel; they weren't looking to make friends. They often failed to meet the owners. On peer-to-peer vehicle rental platforms, one study showed a majority of users preferred *not* to meet the owners.

Perhaps nowhere has the gap between aspirations and realities been so large as in transportation. Environmental benefits were at the core of why even some company founders got into the business. Any way they looked at it, participants in the sharing community saw "shared mobility" as a key component of sustainable transport. Shifting from a system in which most vehicles have single occupants to shared rides would reduce the number of vehicle miles travelled. How could it not be better for the climate? Letting people rent their idle cars to each other increased efficiency and would also reduce ownership, thereby avoiding the embodied emissions of new vehicles. The early discourse promised fewer, fuller vehicles, being used more efficiently, with less total miles driven. Ride-hailing companies were also seen as solutions to longstanding public transport dilemmas such as the last mile problem, or low ridership routes or times. The mantra of access over ownership was premised on the idea that people would readily give up buying personal vehicles, and would be content to rely on other people driving them around. But what has happened?

There is growing evidence that the most important trends in "shared mobility" have been the opposite of what proponents claimed. Commercial ride-hailing came to dominate the field, with shared vehicle ownership and true ridesharing being much smaller segments. Because commercial ride-hailing began with subsidised rides, which have been far lower than traditional taxis, and in some cases, even than public transportation, it has been very popular. Ridership has exploded. Surveys of the US find that people are moving off of public transportation, walking and cycling and onto ride-hailing. They are also choosing to make more trips than they otherwise would. The result is that researchers find that when Uber (the biggest company in the US) arrives in a city, congestion intensifies, vehicle miles travelled rise, and air and carbon pollution increases. New car sales also increase, as drivers buy them to earn on the platform, contrary to claims of "access" over "ownership". They're also a problem for fair access as they have been especially deficient in providing disability access or options for low-income riders. And there's another impact that hasn't been adequately reported: after decades of decline, traffic fatalities are on the rise, a trend that researchers show is causally related to the advent of ride-hailing. Commercial ride-hailing, while initially a boon for consumers, has brought in its wake, a raft of negative ripple effects.

Perhaps most ominously, for-profit ride-hailing platforms are undermining vital public transportation systems, a point Uber finally conceded in its Initial Public Offering documents. They not only pulling people off the public systems. They're eroding political support. Existing research shows that ride-hail passengers are richer, younger, and Whiter than local populations. They disproportionately serve elites. The coalition of middle- and working-class support that underpins public transportation is at risk of splintering.

Does it have to be this way? Is there a better future of "shared mobility" that can actually reduce environmental impacts, serve the needs of residents, and be economically viable? The authors of this excellent new book say yes.

The transportation sector is of vital importance to the human future. Mobility is a central component of well-being; in a modern world it joins food, housing, and education as necessities. It is also crucial because transportation is becoming the largest source of carbon emissions in many places, as electricity production is transitioned to renewables. The "automobile-industrial-complex", built on private ownership of heavy vehicles often occupied by only one person, is problematic because of its spatial demands, pollution and human health impacts, fatalities, and connection to geo-political strife to secure supplies of oil and gas. A shared mobility system built on zero-carbon sources and social justice would help mitigate many of these problems.

To date, the mainstream discussion about transforming the mobility sector has focused on technology. There is boundless excited about autonomous vehicles, apps, geo-location technology, and the like. But as Arcidiacono and Duggan cogently argue, another set of factors will prove to be more important in terms of how the coming mobility system serves people – those having to do with social justice. Unless we put those questions at the centre of the debate, we are at risk of building yet another mobility regime which fails to meet needs and is accompanied by many unintended harms.

Mobility justice should be at the core of ongoing redesign of urban transportation systems. How do we provide a "right to the city?" What do non-elite residents want in terms of mobility? What forms of transport – trains, buses, cycles, walking, scooters? What routes? What times? These are questions that need to be addressed at the most grass-roots level, by the people whose mobility is most constrained. Shared mobility, in the form of technologically advanced systems for providing access, does present many promising options. Apps, dockless systems, just-in-time rides, pooling and shared vehicles will all be part of a new mobility system, with upgraded "public transport" of a conventional type as the backbone. But the design and operation of the transportation future must conform to basic principles of democracy and justice. Continuing down the current path of increasingly privatised options will enhance mobility for elites, but reduce it for the majority of residents.

The urgency of these questions could not be greater. This book is an important contribution to asking and answering them.

Juliet B. Schor

Acknowledgements

This book is the result of research developed over the last three years on the sharing economy and on shared mobility systems. Although the book retraces the theme of sharing mobility in national and international urban contexts, many of the considerations reported have been developed starting from field research activities carried out in the city of Milan and London. In particular, we need to thank: the *Catholic University of the Sacred Heart* and the Centro Studi Modacult which coordinated the survey on the Car2go service in Milan; as well as TraiLab and Collaboriamo with which the research about the BlaBlaCar Community was carried out; the Ambrosianeum Foundation with which a reflection on the theme of innovation on urban mobility was elaborated; LAMA Development and Cooperation Agency with which a feasibility project was developed for a collaborative mobility service in the city of Bologna, in collaboration with the Italian Ministry for Economic Development, and the Uber drivers in London for giving us their time and insights which made up the ethnographic elements of the book.

1 Welcome to the age of sharing

The rise of the sharing economy

Since *The Economist* signalled the *rise of the sharing economy* on its cover in 2013, the notoriety of this reportedly novel form of collaborative economy has increased exponentially. Today, the term "sharing economy" is widely known by the ways that it has redefined how we consume goods and services, and for many it is now simply a part of everyday life for facilitating a broad range of daily practices.

When we talk about the sharing economy, we tend to speak broadly about a new socio-economic model based on collaboration, access, use of idling capacities, and the socialisation of value production facilitated by digital technologies (Botsman and Rogers, 2010; Rifkin, 2014). Nevertheless, as Juliet Schor (2014) warns us, the semantic ambiguity behind the concept of sharing is problematic. She suggests that this umbrella concept covers a sprawling variety of digital platforms and off-line activities, including those facilitated by multinational companies, such as Airbnb, Uber, and Deliveroo, as well as those facilitated by small, local, and informal initiatives of repair and collective exchange such as tool libraries, book clubs, and rail ticket-sharing collectives.

The academic and non-academic debates seem stuck in the so-called "share wars",[1] where efforts are made to separate the "good" sharing economy from the "bad" sharing economy. On the one hand, the sharing economy has been hailed as the future of business and society, praised for its possibility to usher in new forms of life and work (Rifkin, 2014). On the other hand, its ability to blur the lines between life and work, create precarious working conditions, and propel an always-on(line) prosumer lifestyle has called for some to label it as disruptive and damaging to society (Edelman and Luca, 2014; Reich, 2015; Schor and Fitzmaurice, 2015).

The European Commission of the EU offers a useful taxonomy for understanding the spectrum of different ways that the sharing economy has recently been conceptualised.[2] It identifies four ways to distinguish the practices that constitute this economic paradigm:

- The access economy: an economic model involving the exchange of goods and services based on access rather than property.
- The "gig" economy: an economic model based on single or multiple tasks (gigs) activated on request via online platforms or apps.[3]
- The collaborative economy: an economic model in which customers also become producers and form communities.
- The pooling economy: an economic model based on proprietary initiatives or collective management over how transactions take place.

Building on this, The Digital Commons Research Group at the Open University of Catalonia has created a framework that is useful for identifying the differences between what it sees as democratic (or "good") sharing economy platforms and capital-based (or "bad") sharing economy platforms (Fuster Morell and Espelt, 2018). It suggests that democratic platforms operate on the following four principles, which act to separate them from capitalist platforms:

- Governance: there is community involvement in decision-making processes.
- Economy: profitability is not the primary objective. Instead, the project must be sustained through ethical financing, value redistribution, economic transparency, fair payment criteria, and respect for workers' rights.
- Social responsibility: the platform promotes the reduction of environmental impact, the inclusion of socially disadvantaged groups, and inclusive gender/race policies.
- Knowledge and technology: the platform is developed using free/open-source software and distributed technological architecture; algorithms, programmes, and data are transparent; personal data is protected, and all users have a right to the portability of their data.

Running parallel to the debates on its definition and the necessity to distinguish the different forms that the sharing economy takes, other analysis shows the rapid growth of the phenomenon worldwide. According to one regularly cited report by PwC (2015), the European market was expected to be worth 83 billion euros in 2018 and 570 billion euros by 2025. Nevertheless, the levels of participation in the sharing economy are not accurately known, with estimates varying significantly. Andreotti et al. (2017), for example, found that only 18.7% of EU citizens reported having consumed a sharing service. Other studies showed more optimistic rates. For example, it has been estimated that there are 105 million people active in the sharing economy in the US, 14 million in Canada, and 23 million in the UK (Owyang, 2014; Owyang and Samuel, 2015). Studies by Nesta (2014) and the Observatorie de la Confiance (2014) have been some of the most optimistic, suggesting that 60% of people in Britain and almost 50% of people in France already participate in the collaborative economy, respectively. It is Asia however, where the most significant growth is predicted. A study by Nielsen (2013) found that 68% of the Asian-Pacific region were willing to share their assets in a sharing economy, which was contrasted with almost 50% of North Americans and Europeans. The study pointed to China as the country which is set to pioneer the growth of the sharing economy. It suggests that up to 94% of consumers can be expected to become part of the sharing economy in the future. Moreover, the China Council for International Cooperation on Environment and Development (2017) estimates that the sharing economy will grow by an average annual rate of 40% over the next few years. When we look at how far ahead China is in embracing the sharing economy, we can begin to see why these numbers are so high. The popularity of peer-to-peer fintech services such as *Lufax*; umbrella-sharing service, *Molisan*; and the power bank-sharing service, *Shenzhen Laidian* is all illustrative of the kinds of sharing economy services that are prospering in China, but not yet elsewhere. Added to this, we can also see the massive growth in ride- and bike-sharing services that we see all over the world.

The success of the sharing economy is based mainly on an organisational structure which we can call the platform model. This term does not refer simply to a technological infrastructure or a device, but to a new and pervasive economic paradigm that radically reconfigures the organisation of work and consumption in the service economy (Degryse, 2016; Kenney and Zysman, 2016; MIT, 2017). The platform represents a boundaryless organisation based on a core system that engages and coordinates diversified production systems and networks of human and non-human cooperators (Van Dijck et al., 2018). Although platforms distribute and intermediate work, goods, and services, many openly refute their labelling as producers and intermediaries, preferring instead the term of "enablers" to describe their role in facilitating exchanges or sharing between people. We might say that they act as "heterarchies" (Stark, 1996) or "möbius organizations" (Stark and Watkins, 2018) based on the co-optation of assets and resources without any fully formalised constraints. This follows the lean strategies and disruptive philosophies of businesses looking to generate surplus value from efficiency savings in the workforce by leveraging a greater reliance on networked technologies and the labour of consumers. The value of this new economic paradigm is in the enabling of idle capacities and assets, including them in the productive process in what has been defined as an industrious economy where consumers act as "prosumers" (Bruns, 2008; Toffler, 1980). Through this paradigm, the amateur skills of the prosumer become a crucial factor of competitiveness, leading some scholars to talk about the "professional amateur" (Leadbeater and Miller, 2014). In effect, this re-intermediates the relationship between supply and demand and redefines the traditional social and economic barriers of the market.

The platform model, argues Srnicek (2016), has created a new form of capitalism, platform capitalism, where the ultimate goal is profitability generated through the renting of products/services and from digital interactions where data can be extracted and monetised. Nevertheless, along the way the sharing economy has also become part of the strategy for so-called "lifestyle movements" (Haenfler et al., 2012) through which citizen-consumers (Arcidiacono, 2013) try to resist top-down control (De Certau, 1998) by re-embedding the possibilities of this economic model through a proactive and socially conscious use of digital technology (Bennett and Segerberg, 2012), relaunching also the idea of the cooperative platform governance as a viable alternative to platform capitalism (Scholz and Schneider, 2017). In the following chapters of this book, we will examine sharing mobility through the lens of platform capitalism but also through this latter lens of sharing cultures and lifestyles.

Sharing mobility

Sharing mobility, popularised through car and ridesharing services such as Uber, Didi, and BlaBlaCar, but also including micro-transit systems, docked and dockless bicycle-sharing schemes, and scooter services are amongst the most developed of the sharing economy services. Over the past decade, the sector has grown significantly according to international analysis (Owyang and Samuel, 2015). A study by Andreotti et al. (2017), for example, found that 18.2% of consumers in Europe are now users of shared mobility services, which when compared to those using food-sharing (7%) or goods-sharing (7.9%) services represents a significant market.[4]

Following the Observatorio Nazionale Sharing Mobility in Italy (ONSM, 2016: 5), we can define sharing mobility as a socio-economic phenomenon that has affected both the practices of mobility and the consumer attitudes towards mobility. In short, the ONSM characterises sharing mobility as follows:

- The affirmation and diffusion of an extensive and varied number of transport services using digital technologies to facilitate the sharing of vehicles and journeys.
- The ability to create flexible, scalable, and original mobility services.
- The ability to enable interactivity between users/operators and/or collaboration to maximise the use of underutilised mobility assets.

Within the sector today, we can find many types of services; from those that offer different vehicle choices (whether car, scooter, bicycle, or bus), to those that offer different configurations of exchange (e.g. peer-to-peer and on demand), to those that offer alternative types of relationship with customers (e.g. individual or community-based interactions), and those that adopt various business models (e.g. per-trip pricing, hourly rental rate, percentage commissions, etc.). As we will demonstrate in this book, the size and variety of sharing mobility services makes it one of the most fertile test-beds for the sharing economy to experiment in regulation, innovation, and technology (Berger et al., 2014).

Moreover, we might also add that sharing mobility consists of a general behavioural transformation in individuals who tend to favour temporary access to mobility services rather than using their own means of transport. This is a narrative that has been picked up by advocates of sharing mobility as a way to promote these services as technological transport solutions for those that want to reduce their environmental impact. Indeed, sharing mobility has been especially popular amongst those that favour the idea of a smart, sustainable city, where the focus has been on prosocial inclusiveness and environmental sustainability. However, the social and environmental impact of these practices belongs very much to the storytelling that has supported their development. Much research has questioned the virtuous link between the collaborative economy and its environmental and social sustainability, suggesting that it is a form of green- or share-washing (Heinrichs, 2013). This is to say that positive attitudes towards sharing in this context are said to distract us from the mostly technologically deterministic and capitalist ways that many of these services operate.

Despite the recent enthusiasm for sharing mobility facilitated by digital technology, this phenomenon has a long-rooted history in many countries, where it has been a practice of informal social networks between families, neighbours, colleagues, friends, and strangers. For example, *slugging*, which represents early forms of informal ridesharing, became part of urban mobility policies in the 1970s, particularly in US cities such as Washington, Houston, and San Francisco and on the Interstates 95, 66, and 395 between Washington and Northern Virginia. During the 1980s and the 1990s, these practices grew further thanks to the diffusion and evolution of highway technologies and carpooling policies. Nevertheless, the successes of these initiatives were limited by the difficulty in matching itineraries and timetables between commuters (Furuhata et al., 2013). In recent years, with the evolution of communication technologies and especially the diffusion of mobile geo-locatable devices, these difficulties have been largely overcome from a technical perspective. Most notably, they have improved user experience and ultimately ushered in dynamic carpooling and e-hailing to replace casual carpooling and informal vehicle renting.

Mobility as a Service

The recent rise of sharing mobility is also linked to the concept of Mobility as a Service (MaaS), which represents something of a paradigm shift away from the dichotomous concepts of public and private transport. Although there is yet to be a shared universal definition, Kamargianni and Matyas define MaaS as "a user-centric, intelligent mobility distribution model in which all mobility service providers' offerings are aggregated by a sole mobility provider, the MaaS provider, and supplied to users through a single digital platform" (2017: 4). Under this premise, the fragmented mobilities and citizen behaviours of everyday mobility are intended to be unified by a single multimodal service. The MaaS concept aims to overcome these critical elements by reinterpreting the relationship between transport operators, means available and their potential users, sharing of information and access infrastructures, guaranteeing the ideal combination of transport modes, and optimising supply and demand matching.

The promise is that MaaS represents a new ecosystem for mobility that integrates transport operators and providers, data providers, platforms and technology providers, ICT infrastructures, insurance companies, regulatory organisations, and research institutions. In 2015, The

MaaS Alliance was born in Bordeaux, from a public-private partnership involving the Intelligent Transport Society of America and Europe (ITS), with the aim of developing and implementing this paradigm in Europe. Since then, the first experiences of MaaS have been developing in Scandinavia, where ICT-led innovations in environmental sustainability have generally been better supported. In Finland, MaaS Global aims to develop MaaS around the world through the app, Whim. Already active in Helsinki, Whim offers three types of subscription: monthly passes giving unlimited usage of all public transport, taxis, and car- and bike-sharing services; 30 days prepaid passes with full access to public transport and limited access to private sharing mobility services; and pay-as-you-go style passes. Other MaaS initiatives that allow similar integrated access to public/private travel services include UbiGo in Gothenburg, Sweden, and Go in Denver, US.

These experiments show how MaaS is also an experiment in novel forms of mobility management strategy, which are designed to appeal to the dynamism of urban mobility practices. MaaS recognises the diversity of mobility practices and understands that transport solutions are not universal, but instead should take a networked approach that accounts for the specific needs of different citizens, at different spatial and temporal scales. For this reason, the concept of MaaS directly relates to contemporary sharing mobility, which is interested in using networked technologies to find dynamic multimodal solutions to the issues of transport. This is also the reason why sharing mobility services have become an integral part of the MaaS concept and a key area for policymakers and mobility providers interested in MaaS to focus on.

Nevertheless, whilst MaaS has been designed with public mobility goals in mind, large parts of the sharing mobility sector have become key to the development of platform capitalism over the past decade (Srnicek, 2016), where the primary goals of acquiring users, generating revenues, and (eventually) profit are different. Using Srnicek's taxonomy of digital platforms, we can see that many of today's sharing mobility services fall into two categories – *product platforms* and *lean platforms*. The former includes car-sharing services such as Zipcar and Drive Now and bike-/scooter-sharing services such as Ofo and Lime, where revenues and profits are generated by transforming products into services that can be rented. The latter includes ridesharing services such as Uber, Lyft, Ola, Didi, and carpooling service BlaBlaCar, where revenues and profits are generated by mediating the interactions between riders and drivers and by keeping running costs low through owning as few assets as possible.[5] Unlike other models of sharing mobility, such as those services focused on supporting localised peer-to-peer transactions (e.g. localised carpooling), public transportation, fixed-dock bike sharing, and informal sharing cultures, we suggest that *sharing mobility platforms* (product and lean) can be characterised as a model that seeks profitability and growth over sustainable solutions to social and environmental transportation issues. As we shall see, sharing mobility platforms have become particularly problematic for city transportation planners and regulators because their fundamental goals are markedly different. Though this is not a strict binary, the former tend to be interested in creating efficient transport solutions for profit, whilst the latter are interested in managing the movement of people.

Exploring the impacts of sharing mobility: outlining the book

Much of the current analysis on sharing mobility has focused on emerging technologies and service design (Agatz et al., 2012; Furuhata et al., 2013) or on its traffic and environmental impacts (Chan and Shaheen, 2012; Ferguson, 1997; Global e-Sustainability Initiative, 2008; Kelley, 2007). There is less work that explores the socio-economic impact of sharing mobility (Mazzella and Sandurarajan, 2016; Novaco and Collier, 1994), and even fewer studies that focus on the broad spectrum of sharing mobility (i.e. not just the well-known Silicon Valley companies). The many cases of success, but also failures demonstrated by sharing mobility companies around inclusion, exclusion, and exploitation in specific local contexts suggest there is a need for a sociological approach to investigate how such mobility forms play out in the realities of everyday life.

The purpose of this book is therefore to examine and evaluate sharing mobility from a sociological perspective; to explore sharing mobility as a socio-economic and socio-technical phenomenon rather than as a purely technological or engineering innovation. Cumulatively, the chapters in this book seek to unravel some of the myriad of ways that sharing mobilities are impacting on contemporary life; from how we get around, to who is using these services, to whom are they aimed at, to what extent they are sustainable, and for whom do they benefit financially. We are also concerned with questions of how cities around the world are approaching the growth of sharing mobility, how these services are changing employment practices, and what motivates people to sign up for these services. Sharing mobility has become part of everyday urban life for many people, and yet in its current guise we cannot say that it is for everyone. As we will demonstrate in this book, many of the well-known services simply do not constitute a set of transport options that are accessible, affordable, or inclusive for all citizens. However, we do think that the premise of sharing mobility has great potential to be all of these if it is situated differently – displaced from platform capitalism – as services that embrace cultural practices of sharing and reciprocity.

This makes sharing mobility a key part of the perennial urban question of how to create livable cities for all. We know that the ability to move in metropolitan space-time is a key indicator of well-being for urban citizens (Boltanski and Chiappello, 1999) and therefore represents a crucial area of policy in urban planning (Fainstein, 2001). We also know that cities around the world are growing and changing to incorporate larger populations and a diversity of practices and mobility flows. Decentralisation, outsourcing, tertiarisation, flexible working, urban sprawl, and the fragmentation of social life are just some of the variables that have contributed to the growth of flows towards and within cities. Over time, these changes have led to increased traffic congestion and pollution, but also to social inequalities and exclusionary transport policy. Following the notion that cities are actors and spaces for social innovation (Purcell, 2002), these changes already, and will continue to, require new forms of mobility that can meet these changes. Sharing mobility services are already providing innovations that meet some of these challenges, but much more could be done to make these actions socially responsible and environmentally sustainable.

To talk about the relationship between the city and innovation means to talk less and less about *Smart Cities* and more and more about *Sharing Cities* (McLaren and Agyeman, 2015). This is especially the case in those urban contexts that propose themselves as leaders and enablers of new forms of entrepreneurship based on the production of services through the platform paradigm, such as San Francisco, Seoul, London, Amsterdam, or Milan. At a time when the city is rethinking mobility and redefining transport policies, sharing mobility represents a strategic lever with the potential to impact positively on sustainability and urban livability, but this needs to be acted on by technologists, policymakers, regulators, and citizens alike.

With this in mind, we adopt and adapt the sociological concept of *the right to the city* (Lefebvre, 1968), which we define as a collective right for urban inhabitants to have a meaningful influence, free from state or corporate interests, in the decisions and processes that shape the public spaces and practices of their lives, as a starting point to analyse the impacts of sharing mobility and its potential future. At a time when platform capitalism continues to enfold the sharing economy, we suggest this framework has never been more relevant for pursuing alternative ways of realising the potential of sharing mobility. Mobility has played a crucial role in the history of the right to the city concept in that it is based on two pillars, the right to participation and the right to appropriation, and yet mobility is rarely attended to explicitly as a key component of the right to the city movements (Middleton, 2018; Verlinghieria and Venturini, 2018). In response to this, we use the book to argue that the right to the city must also be studied and fought for in and through our everyday mobilities, which increasingly unfold through a spectrum of shared mobile practices.

The book continues with a chapter outlining the history and global context from which sharing mobility emerges, before going on to describe and analyse the different forms of sharing mobility in different contexts. The analysis will use a series of studies (Bardhi and Eckhardt, 2012; Handke and Jonuschat, 2013; Martin and Shaheen, 2011; ONSM, 2016; Shaheen et al., 2006) to discuss how different histories and socio-institutional contexts have affected the successes and failures of sharing mobility, and how these factors have affected issues relating to transport regulation, inter-modality, urban accessibility, and economic and environmental sustainability.

The following chapter introduces the notion of the right to the city and argues why it is important and increasingly relevant for understanding contemporary urban mobilities. After tracing the origins and key theoretical ideas of the term from the social sciences, the chapter argues that a truly civil society – a society and a city for all – will require that we rethink not only the possibilities for public spaces, but also the possibilities of shared mobilities. It will suggest that in light of the so-called sharing economy, the right to the city and its forms of shared mobilities are at risk of being engulfed by individualised and profit-driven forms of civility, when the core principles and ideals of sharing mobility (evangelised but rarely practiced in this sector) could lead us in a different direction, towards more inclusive and just urban mobilities.

Drawing from global case studies of transportation and labour regulation and from ethnographic fieldwork in London, the next chapter examines the socio-economic intersections that emerge from new forms of shared mobility. It will examine issues of regulation, labour, and data, which are becoming increasingly relevant around the world, with Uber and other ridesharing companies having been accused of promoting unfair competition, exploiting workers, and perpetuating existing social inequalities. This chapter will assess whether the so-called uberisation of urban mobility has the potential to reduce the positive social and economic impact of sharing mobility, and put forward the notion of *relational regulation* as a way to address these challenges.

The following chapter explores the relational impact of sharing mobility. The sharing economy is often discussed as a re-socialising practice of economic exchange. In all forms of sharing mobility, such relations produce very different meanings and outcomes, which inevitably have various impacts on those involved. In car or bike sharing, the relational dimension is not an explicit feature of the service. It is only in the everyday market interactions between the company and the user(s) of the service that these relations are realised, for instance, between a driver and a passenger. Conversely, for sharing platforms these complex economic and socio-spatial interactions are only ever revealed through basic interactions with software applications, such as the popular star rating (Uber) and rewards systems (Lyft). As a result, there is a significant difference between the ways that users experience shared mobilities and the ways that data is collected and used to improve the experiences of shared mobilities. Brand affiliation, community identity, and shared rituals, for example, are not well represented by the simplicity implied in most digital ratings systems. Such relations are key factors in the innovation of the mobility service, and they are heavily linked to the design of the platform or with the boundaries between work and non-work, or the functioning of reputation algorithms. This chapter will examine several case studies from around the world and provide analysis on specific platforms to demonstrate how these factors could be crucial for the success of sharing mobility (Bruglieri, 2018; Manzella and Sundararajan, 2016).

In our conclusion, we attempt to analyse the most prominent impacts of sharing mobility, to assess its current limitations and potential applications. In doing so, we provide some recommendations for policymakers, transport and labour regulators, technologists, and users interested in realising the potential of sharing mobility as evolutionary system of mobility that can support our right to mobility justice in the city.

Ultimately, this book aims to provide an up to date sociological analysis of sharing mobility by emphasising the relationality of its practices and impacts. We aim to highlight how this emerging phenomenon is affecting our mobility practices inasmuch as it is affecting our everyday social lives, urban politics and environmental concerns. It is therefore a book intended for a wide audience, where we hope it will be useful for policymakers, transport planners, regulators, technologists, academics, and the wider public interested in the changing nature of urban mobility.

Notes

1 www.shareable.net/how-platform-coops-can-beat-death-stars-like-uber-to-create-a-real-sharing-economy/.
2 www.eesc.europa.eu/resources/docs/com2016-356-final.pdf.
3 Developing this further, Frenken et al. (2015) suggest that in order to distinguish the sharing economy from the often associated practices of *on-demand services* or the *gig-economy*, a genuine sharing economy must be defined as an economy based on the temporary exchange of physical assets between individuals (known as consumer-to-consumer) and not by the service exchanges between businesses (b2b) or between businesses and consumers (business-to-consumer). However, this type of definition can be restrictive because consumers can feasibly share more than their assets with each other. Time banks, for example, are based on the consumer-to-consumer exchange of time and not physical assets.
4 Comparatively, 18.6% of consumers in the same study were said to be users of sharing accommodation services.
5 Nevertheless, Uber does own the vehicles testing its self-driving car software, which suggests that the future model of Uber could shift to one where it does own a fleet of vehicles.

2 The successes and failures of shared urban mobility

Going beyond the distinction between public and private mobility

As argued by Castells (1989), society has emerged as a *space of flows* in which the modernisation process (Harvey, 1990; Urry, 2000) aided by technological innovations have increased public and private mobility and reduced their costs. At the same time, emerging societal and environmental pressures have led us towards a rethinking of mobility. This tension, emblematic of the kind of contradiction that characterises globalisation today, can be linked to three trends that should be taken into account: population growth and increasing urbanisation, global car cultures, and an awareness of the environmental impacts of transport. Taken together these trends seem to push an increasingly educated and environmentally aware world further towards a future of fossil-fuelled urban automobility.

First, the world's population continues to grow, albeit with unequal rhythms (UN, 2017). The so-called "global south", especially countries in Africa, has had the greatest growth in recent years, instead of countries in Asia where growth has been slower. This is accompanied by a progressive aging of the population, given that life expectancy has gone globally from 67.2 years in 2000 to 70.8 years in 2017.[1] Likewise, the growing number of single-person households and specific life/work needs puts a stronger emphasis on individual mobility practices.

Second, an emerging cultural transformation has changed our attitudes towards private and collective mobility. The rise of mass motorisation that represented a symbol of emancipation to Fordist societies (Gartman, 2004; McCarthy, 2007; Miller, 2001; Wells and Beynon, 2011) is still representative of a positional asset (a status symbol) today (Nelissen and Meijers, 2011). However, the density and complexity of urban social life in recent decades have contributed to a growing hostility towards private

14 *Successes and failures*

motorisation and the progressive values that have historically underpinned it (Hiscock et al., 2002). And yet, private motorisation is still growing, especially in BRICS countries (such as China and India), but also in the Western countries, which were the first to know mass motorisation.

Generationally, younger people seem to register ambivalent attitudes towards the car property. In particular, so-called "millennials" are said to be the symbol of a new culture of mobility. Studies show that this generation is less dependent on cars than previous generations (around 10%–15% less), while they are much more intensive users of public transport, especially in urban contexts, where multiple transportation options are available (Dutzik et al., 2014; Engels and Liu, 2011; Sivak and Schoettle, 2012; TransitCenter, 2014; ULI, 2013).[2] This is not necessarily their choice, but instead reflects the increasingly precarious lifestyles of this group (Wells and Xenias, 2015) where the private car represents a cost that is difficult to sustain or is simply out of reach. The rise of smart-working also modifies the need for mobility within this segment of the population. As much of this work tends to be concentrated in the city where regulation is increasingly restrictive on the use of private cars, the eco-efficiency and the benefits/costs are outweighed by those of using public or shared transport.

The dependence of private car mobility is strongly differentiated in the major cities of the world (Rode et al., 2017). If we compare the cities with the highest level of GDP per capita, the use of private vehicles reaches between 80% and 90% of trips in some North American cities, compared to less than 15% in Asian cities like Tokyo or Hong Kong, and it is much more contained in big European cities like London, Berlin, or Paris, which in recent years have increased their "car-free zones" and zero emissions policies. In the same way, the number of cars per 1,000 inhabitants varies significantly between the city (ibid.). For example, Italy has about 600 cars per 1,000 inhabitants, similar to that of much larger countries such as Australia (about 556) and Germany (517), while in countries like Brazil the amount is 179 per 1,000 inhabitants, and in China about 44 per 1,000 inhabitants. However, by 2025 the growth of automobiles will be the highest in urbanising economies like China and Brazil rather than North America or Europe (World Bank, 2014).

The rise of this "post-automobility" or "de-motorisation" age has led to a drop in car sales in many mature western markets (Cohen, 2012). This has affected the automotive sector's business strategies, where there has been a shift from a supply of cars to the supply of services related to cars (financial services, assistance, and maintenance, insurance, etc.). The choice of Volvo to not exhibit any cars on its stands during the 2018 International Motor Show in Los Angeles is representative of this strategical shift. As a Volvo manager, Michele Crisci, commented,

> we want the public to look at us not as simple vendors of cars but as a partner offering mobility services...the concept that we present in Los Angeles, that is to shift the focus on mobility itself, is worth more than the car.[3]

Third, the growth of private mobility has had significant environmental impacts, especially in urban areas. In a recent report by Greenpeace, the current mobility system is said to be one of the greatest sources of global air pollution and also one of the greatest consumers of natural resources (Hickman et al., 2017). According to IEA reports (2009, 2012), 30% of produced energy is used for transport, and by 2050 it is said that urban mobility systems will use 17.3% of the planet's capacities, which is five times more than in 1990 (Little, 2015). Furthermore, it is estimated that the construction of roads and other automotive infrastructures account for between 25% and 40% of land use in urban areas compared with 10% in rural areas (OECD, 2006). Large and medium cars are said to be the main contributors of air pollution in cities with the amount of CO_2 grams per passenger/km produced being 312 and 191, respectively, against the 185 produced by local buses or 50 by the Metro (Rode et al., 2017). Recently, the German Federal Environment Agency certified that road transport is responsible for about two-thirds of the nitrogen dioxide emissions in German city centres (Berger et al., 2014). A World Bank study (Darido et al., 2009) showed how in the biggest Chinese cities like Beijing and Guangzhou, carbon emissions from transport were growing between 4% and 6% a year. In Shanghai, they grow by a staggering 15% every year. These data demonstrate how private mobility has become a "global emergency" from an environmental point of view. During the 2016 UN Global Conference in Ashgabat, it was stressed how in many cities across the world public transport remains "unsustainable, unsafe, inefficient, inaccessible or unaffordable". This was just the latest in a series of warnings around transport and emissions. We could also include the European Commission's (2011) White Paper of transport which highlights the need to change our current path towards a more sustainable mobility and the recommendations of the UN's Paris Climate Agreement (2015).

With this evidence in mind, there is a need for a paradigm shift in our conception of mobility. In essence, we must push towards the creation of a new urban ecosystem that overcomes the dichotomy between private and public mobility. Sharing mobility is considered an innovative way to respond to these challenges because it is based on the need to guarantee

16 Successes and failures

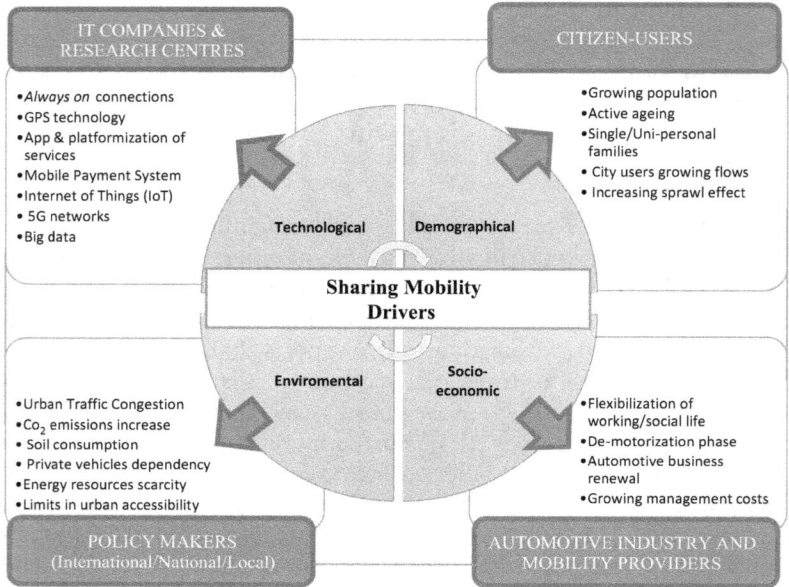

Figure 2.1 Sharing mobility ecosystem

flexible, scalable, and sustainable services that meet the increasingly complex demands of urban populations (see Figure 2.1). By creating a sharing alliance between private individuals and professional operators around the oversupply of vehicles (cars, bikes, scooters, etc.), these services offer the real possibility of a public/private transportation network that could help to address to the contemporary issues of urban mobility.

Fifteen shades of sharing

Sharing mobility services are a set of diverse operators and solutions (see Figure 2.2). First of all, we must distinguish between sharing a vehicle and sharing a ride. At the same time, it is necessary distinguish *vertical service delivery systems,* for which a company provides the vehicles and defines the price of sharing, and *collaborative delivery systems*, which are based on a horizontal and disintermediated process of exchange and peer-to-peer transactions. Vehicle-sharing systems can be classified as follows:

- *Station-based*, for which the vehicle is picked up and deposited in special predefined parking bays and organised in some strategic

Successes and failures   17

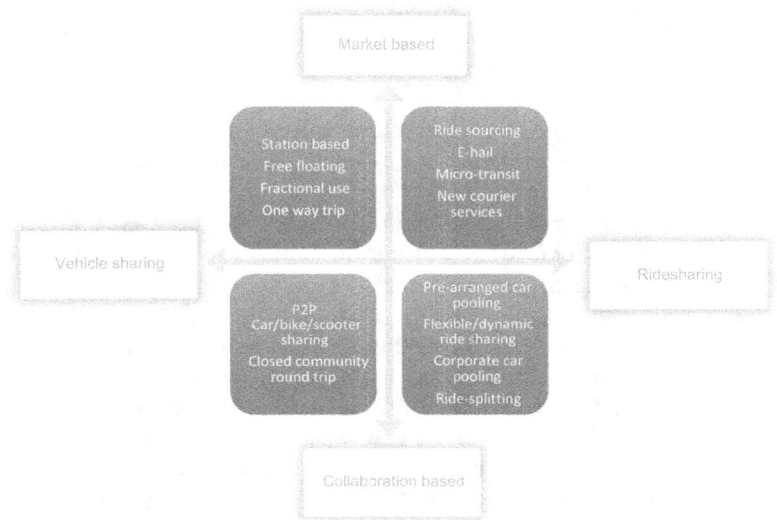

Figure 2.2 Types of sharing mobility

points of the city. Co-Wheels in the UK, Autolib in France, Exchange in Germany and Belgium, Zipcar in the US, Orix in Japan, and EVCard in China are all examples of this model.
- *Free-floating*, where vehicles can be picked up and parked freely within the urban area where the service is active. These systems include large global companies such as Car2go (15,000 vehicles shared in 40 cities worldwide) and DriveNow (5,500 vehicles shared in seven European countries), as well as smaller local providers like Enjoy (Italy), GreenMobility (Denmark), Communauto (Canada, France), EduoAuto and E-Car (China). Cooperative car-sharing services such as Yea! (France) and the Saskatoon Carshare Co-operative (Canada) also operate free-floating models.

Vehicle-sharing systems may also be differentiated according to the type of use. We identify three categories here:

- *Roundtrip vehicle sharing* is when a fleet is used for round trips that require users to pay by hour. This form has been used by the employees of some multinationals, such as Alpha City or Enterprise

Car Share. Smaller, community-based schemes have also been popular in rural regions which are lacking adequate public transport. For example, numerous schemes developed and supported by Co-Wheels have emerged across Scotland over the past decade (Gleave, 2018).
- *One-way sharing* is where vehicles are used for point-to-point trips. This is more typical of public-sharing services such as docked bike-sharing schemes.
- *Fractional ownership*, a hybrid of roundtrip and one-way sharing, has been introduced by automobile companies to facilitate the shared leasing of vehicles. Ford Motor Company, for example, announced a leasing pilot programme that enables three to six people to lease a vehicle together. Nissan, Porsche, and Mercedes have also launched various initiatives based on this approach, which include tiered subscription services that enable access to multiple vehicle types. This new way of conceiving mobility attracts traditional automotive players, but also new start-ups like Orto, in London, where the focus is on developing a luxury car leasing service.

In the majority of cases, vehicle sharing is predominantly a system in which no user is the exclusive owner of the vehicle. Instead, it is made available and maintained by a company supplier. A "negative reciprocity" mechanism prevails, because only one actor (in this case the company) takes over the greater economic benefits generated by the transaction (Bardhi and Eckardt, 2012).

In the early 2000s, the first cases of *peer-to-peer car sharing* such as Rentmycar (2001) and Autopia (2004) began to emerge. The real exponential growth of this model was during the recent economic crisis with the emergence of services such as Auting in Italy, Tamyca in Germany, BlueMove in Spain, VoitureLibe in France, Turo in the US, and Movo and PPZuche in China. Peer-to-peer car sharing is very different from traditional car rental systems because it is based on the relations between users, who tend to collaborate by dividing the means and costs of rides. As these services tend to operate on the basis of non-recurring trips and single rides without fixed time schedules, users coordinate trips through instant messaging, websites, and apps. The mechanism that is generated is a "positive reciprocity", in which the two subjects, drivers and passengers, obtain advantages in terms of reducing the monetary and/or time costs of a trip, while also contributing to the reduction of traffic congestion, pollution, and consumption of fossil fuels.

The *ridesharing* (sometimes called ride-hailing) that is popular today combines some of the characteristics of peer-to-peer and one-way sharing, but its basic principles can also be seen throughout the history of hitchhiking, slugging, and casual carpooling, which were experimented within the American metropolises during the 1970s. It was however the emergence of *pre-arranged carpooling* where the origins of today's technologically mediated ridesharing can be traced to. An example of this is the *vanpooling* services provided by companies such as 3M and Chrysler in the US in the 1970's, which arranged journeys for commuters travelling to/from work. Nevertheless, these first forms of carpooling were usually based on neighbours or company colleagues and were limited to specific locations or circumstances, which were difficult to replicate elsewhere (Furuhata et al., 2013).

With the development of internet and mobile GPS systems, pre-arranged carpooling systems have been overtaken by *dynamic* or *flexible carpooling* (e.g. BlaBlaCar) that are able to guarantee instantaneous matching between passengers and drivers, optimise routes, and give accurate waiting/journey times. With flexible/dynamic carpooling, users are even more independent and autonomous, effectively disintermediating the role previously played by centralised institutions (Agatz et al., 2012; Amey et al., 2011; Burris and Winn, 2006). In this scenario, rides can be taken for both short and long distances and ride matching is an automated process based on algorithmic processes. Furuhata et al. (2013) suggest four ways in which these automated processes have become central to carpooling:

- Routing and time: routing and scheduling of rides is automated in order to respond to specific requests.
- Pairing driver and rider(s): mainly in terms of locations and times.
- Keywords list and bulletin boards: the request and offer, traceable and searchable using predefined term.
- First-come first-serve principle: there is no pre-arrangement supported by the ride-matching system.

Automated matching extends to an indefinite number of users and can also be classified by the type of mobility need (extra-urban, urban, or dedicated to reach specific events, such as a concert or football match, etc.). For this matching system to work well, there needs to be adequate supply of drivers for the demand of riders, which means that both riders and drivers need to be incentivised to take part. These incentives are usually economic, with both wanting to use the service as a way to save money on transport. In some cases, we have seen services starting out with community sharing aims developing profitability aims. These services are no longer characterised by the sharing of the trips to reduce costs, but instead become characterised by a traditional economic transaction in which the price is determined by the digital platforms that mediate the interactions between cars and rider requests.

These changes have transformed carpooling into ride-sourcing systems, or more widely known as *ridesharing* systems, which is a relatively new concept that builds on the taxi model of transporting passengers' door to door by extending two specific features:

- Journeys are arranged, processed, paid for, and rated exclusively through the use of smartphone technology.
- Drivers are considered independent contractors rather than employees and are not required to have a professional taxi licence to do the job.

Ridesharing has by far the biggest market share of sharing mobility and includes services such as Uber (worldwide) and Lyft (North America), which have grown exponentially over the past decade to the point where, until recently, Uber had been valued at a staggering $120 billion (Hoffman et al., 2018). Moreover, major metropolitan areas are the main catchment and development area for the ridesharing systems around the world. Taking the US case as an example, according to data made available by the Federal Highway Administration (2018), of the approximately 1,739,000 rides exchanged in 2017, about 70% were taken in the nine largest metropolitan areas of the country (Boston, Chicago, Los Angeles, Miami, Philadelphia, San Francisco, Seattle, and Washington DC, New York) with New York as the leading market in which almost one-fifth of sharing mobility journeys were made by ride-sourcing platforms.

These digitally mediated systems are phenomenon that has inspired a process of innovation in traditional taxi services across the world, which have now adopted so-called e-hailing apps (like MyTaxi or WeTaxi, active in different European cities, or Hailo in UK, Goehail in New York, Careem Networks in Dubai), carpooling, and ride-splitting services (such as Uber POOL or Lyft Line). This type of innovation has also modified traditional collective transport such as Shuttle services or small vans (so-called Micro-transit) making them even more customisable and referring to specific targets of customers (tourists, small removals, commuters, users of airport services, medical patients, etc.), provided by companies such as Chariot, Via, or Ubeeqo. Equally interesting is the hybridisation between collaborative and market services of the new Courier Network Services (CNS) that provide delivery services of different kinds of items (food, gits, flowers, packages, documents, etc.) by connecting shippers and customers through an online app or platform using peer-to-peer schemes, like Postmates or Instacart.

All of these services of ride or delivery sharing will evolve and develop even further with the advent of the driverless technology, if or when it arrives. Therefore, it is not surprising that the major private operators of sharing mobility (such as Uber or Lyft, for example) are engaged in substantial investments in autonomous driving and are building partnerships with the major IT and automotive companies such as Volvo, Volkswagen, General Motors, and FCA.

Sharing mobility: a history of peaks, troughs, and *resurrections*

Ciari and Becker (2017) suggest that the first car-sharing experiences date back to 1947 with the Sefage programme (Selbstfahrergemeinschaft), started in Zurich. Although the programme ran until 1998, the idea quickly became outdated by the expansion of mass motorisation that exploded after the Second World War. Similar programmes with varying degrees of success spread throughout Europe between 1970 and 2000 (Shaheen and Cohen, 2008). These included Procotip (France, 1971–1973), Witkar (Amsterdam, Netherlands, 1974–1988), Green Cars (UK, 1977–1984), Bilpoolen (Lund, Sweden, 1976–1979), Vivallabil (Orebro, Sweden, 1983–1998), and Bilkooperativ (Gothenburg, Sweden, 1985–1990). In the US, similar services were developed, but short lived: The Mobility Enterprise programme, developed within Purdue University ran between 1983 and 1986, and the San Francisco STAR case from 1983 to 1985. As Shaheen et al. (2009) show, there was also a period of experimentation in car sharing across America, which focused on a neighbourhood residential model, between the 1990s and the 2000s. However, the real boom in the US occurred in the second half of the 2000s, with the arrival of many operators and the experimentation of new technologies such as smartcards and key fobs for vehicle entry, or GPS for vehicle tracking. A symbol of this success is exemplified by the case of Zipcar, whose founder, Robin Chase, pioneered the American revival of car sharing from 2000 onwards after being inspired by the first experiences of European car sharing. Initially underestimated by the big American automotive and traditional transport providers, the company achieved steady growth in several cities such as Washington, San Francisco, and New York, to the point of being listed on the stock exchange (Iacovini, 2014). In 2013, the company was bought by the vehicle rental company, AVIS, and has since entered markets across North America and Europe. The current phase of car sharing sees the American market as one of the most promising for the service and is increasingly impacting the way of thinking about urban mobility management policies through the development of cooperation between different operators and through fiscal or political incentives, like dedicated spaces for parking shared vehicles.

A similar story can be seen in the growth of bike-sharing services, which developed initially in Europe before becoming established across the world. The first experiments in bike sharing took place in Amsterdam around the 1960s with the introduction of "White Bikes". The idea came from a Dutch anarchist group with strong ecological sensitiveness, called Provo, who had distributed leaflets announcing the end of the "motorized bourgeoisie's asphalt kingdom". As a form of participatory activism, the group painted several bikes white and left them around the city for people to use freely. The experiment failed almost immediately, as without adequate public regulation and technological systems able to exert some form of stringent control, bikes were seized by the police, stolen or vandalised. Nevertheless, this case led to bike-sharing schemes organised by docking stations and the need to pay a deposit to unlock the bike. The first systems of this type were installed in Copenhagen in 1995, but it wasn't until 1998 when France introduced the IT-based system, Vélo à la Carte, that the real revolution was realised. In the same year, it also arrived in the US (in cities like Portland and Boulder) where experiences were motivated by a strong environmental and community spirit. The Boulder service, for example, was deliberately inspired by the early Dutch experience with an active involvement of high school volunteers and a completely free of charge service. As happened in the first experiences of the 1960s, even these early American experimentations proved unsustainable due to the impact of theft and vandalism.

The real boom came in 2001, when many services and payment systems were digitalised. These changes led to service that was easily scalable and replicable around the world. This technological phase represented an important flywheel for the spread of bike sharing in Southeast Asia, in cities such as Singapore, Chjangwon, and Wuhan, which has since become one of the most important markets for bike sharing. Today the main free-floating bike sharing operators in the world are Chinese, with companies like Mobike and Ofo dominating the market not only in China but also around the world in cities such as London and Paris.

Conversely, the origins of carpooling practices are not to be found in Europe but rather in the US. The first example was the Car-sharing Club, led by the US government, as a way to save fuel during the Second World

War. Then, during the years of the oil shock in the 1970s, the practice was reprised as governments and citizens sought cheaper means of car transport. As Handke and Jonuschat (2013) suggest, oil prices, suburbanisation, inefficient public transport, and a concentration of workplaces in downtown areas were all contributing factors that explain the American transition from informal carpooling towards pre-arranged carpooling during this time. In addition to this, people were encouraged to travel together by government-backed schemes such as HOV (highly occupied vehicles) lanes for cars with more than one occupant, which proved to be especially successful for suburban commuters in Washington DC, Los Angeles, and San Francisco seeking less congested routes to work and back. We might say that this form of ridesharing was an institutionalised version of hitchhiking that, as also noted for the first experiences of bike sharing, did not come at any great expense except for the inexpensive lane toll that could be shared amongst drivers and passengers. The growth and popularity of HOV lanes was eventually affected by the end of the oil crisis, as crude oil prices returned to normal. However, the carpooling mechanisms developed during this time remain key to mobility management strategies in many large American cities. In particular, the origins of databases for the organisation and optimisation of the supply and demand matching can be traced back to this time.

In Europe, carpooling arrived in the second half of the 1980s, encouraged by the spread of the practice in the North American cities. However, in the beginning these schemes had limited success and failed to persuade large numbers of people to participate. This is partly because those who subscribed to these services paid a fee to those organising it while the users shared the expenses with the trip mates. Services of this type reappeared with new force in the US with Zimride, in 2007, but also in other contexts such as Grab in Southeast Asia, Ola in India, and BlaBlaCar in Europe. In these cases, mobile technology has helped to improve usability by providing flexible and real-time solutions, which in turn has helped facilitate the transition from carpooling to ride-sourcing and e-hailing services.

This latter form of sharing mobility exists in a grey area between licensed and informal transport services. They represent significant new entrants in the mobility market, especially in the ways that they have disrupted taxi markets, undercut competition, and challenged existing regulation. In some cases, these services have been officially recognised and framed legally as Transportation Network Companies (TNC), as was the case in California, in 2013. In other cases, these services have been banned and considered illegal by national judges (see Chapter 4). These services have also started to expand in

24 *Successes and failures*

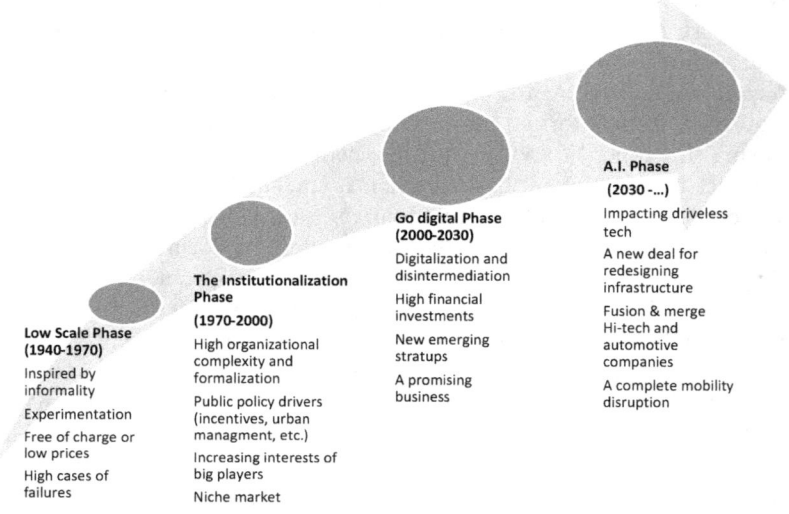

Figure 2.3 Historical evolution of shared mobility

developing low- to medium-income countries. Motorbike ridesharing taxis such as Safemotos in Rwanda and Safeboda in Kenya are becoming popular in these countries, as is long distance car ridesharing (e.g. Dichungtaxi in Vietnam) and specialised services such as Ojek Syar'I, an Indonesian taxi ridesharing service operated by and for Muslim women (Institute for Sustainable Future, 2017).

In conclusion, we can characterise the history of sharing mobility under four distinct phases (see Figure 2.3):

1 Localised phase (1940–1980): an experimental and informal model of sharing mobility organised at a local level. In many cases, participation in sharing mobility during this phase was incentivised by low or no cost for participation. Proximity to other users and a local knowledge of how to participate produced a sense of belonging to a specific urban or sub-urban community. In effect, this local phase was often based on communal values over the ecological impact of mobility and a sense of collective identity, which bonded these communities together. However, there is evidence to suggest that this phase produced fragmented experiences for users, and there were difficulties in terms of scalability and service dysfunctions (for example, high rates of vandalism and theft).

2 Institutionalisation phase (1990–2000): sharing mobility practices are formalised and organised in a structured manner inspiring public policies and mobility management systems. During this phase, the most important companies in the transport, automotive, and logistics sectors are starting to take an interest in the issue and they start to develop their own offerings. However, these initiatives are little more than a vanguard at this stage resulting in a relatively a niche market.

3 Going digital phase (2000–2030): technological innovation revives and renews sharing mobility. Services become more dynamic, interactive, and flexible thanks to the rise of intermediary digital technologies including the smartphone and location-based technology. The presence of big players, above all the automotive industry, and the influence of technology start-ups is strengthened by major financial investment. The result is a market that is maturing, expanding, and segmenting to suit the needs and interests of a range of people. The communitarian principles of phase one are incorporated or hybridised with utilitarian-economic motivations, and we begin to see these services scale massively around the globe.

4 A.I. phase (2030–…): the next phase will take shape as the introduction and implementation driverless technology begins to proliferate. There is potential here for a real cultural revolution in shared mobility, but it will need a significant "new deal" to redesign transport infrastructures that is based on a strong public and private partnership. Advocates for autonomous vehicle technologies suggest that they will be available in the next 10/20 years. These are likely to be based on a *vehicle-to-vehicle* (V2V) and *vehicle-to-infrastructure* (V2I) connection systems, establishing new forms of interaction between drivers and vehicles, but also between drivers and the surrounding environment via the Internet of Things (IoT). This revolution has the potential to completely modify habits and practices, and consequently the whole range of services and markets connected to mobility (insurance, payment systems, parking services, etc.).

A market with great potential?

Data on the global dissemination and potential of sharing mobility systems are very fragmented and often difficult to compare. The main sources can be derived from the consulting sector (for example, research reports from Deloitte, McKinsey, Market and Research, and

Roland Berger) or the financial sector (for example, Goldmann-Sachs, Ark Investments, Merryll Lynch, and Bank of America). Supplementing this is a growing body of academic literature from research centres such as the Transportation Sustainability Research Center (TSRC) at the University of Berkeley, and research from public institutions, like l'Agence de l'Environnement et de la Maîtrise de l'Énergie (ADEME) in France.

Most of these data converge around the potential of sharing mobility to achieve positive market growth. According to estimates made by Merill-Lynch and Bank of America (2018), vehicles used for sharing mobility services increased from 17 m to 22 m between 2015 and 2016 and are expected to continue to grow to 130 m by 2030, representing the 8% of all vehicles used. According to data from the Research and Markets Report (2018), the Mobility as a Service (MaaS) system (see Chapter 1) is expected to grow from $38.76 billion in 2017 to $358.35 billion by 2025. Figure 2.4 shows a projection of these estimates made by ARK-Investment (Keeney, 2017) until 2035. MaaS attracts mainly large investors and large industrial groups linked to automotive and high-end technology companies. For this reason, MaaS has become an attractive market for young start-ups seeking investment (see Figure 2.5). Of the main start-ups funded by investment funds and business angels in 2016, 44.5% is related to sharing mobility services, especially in emerging countries such as Asia, where it represents almost 60% of start-ups in the mobility sector, in Latin America, where it represents almost 47%, and in Africa where it exceeds 50% (Canales et al., 2017).

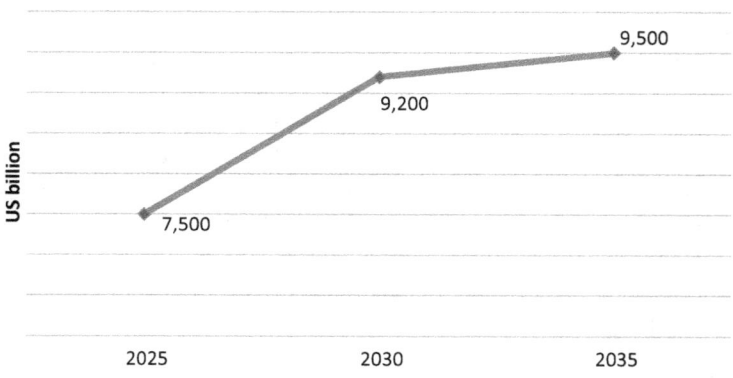

Figure 2.4 Estimated mobility as a service (MaaS) market capitalisation worldwide from 2025 to 2035 (in billions of US dollars)
Source: Our elaboration on data of Keeney (2017) for Ark Investment Research

Successes and failures 27

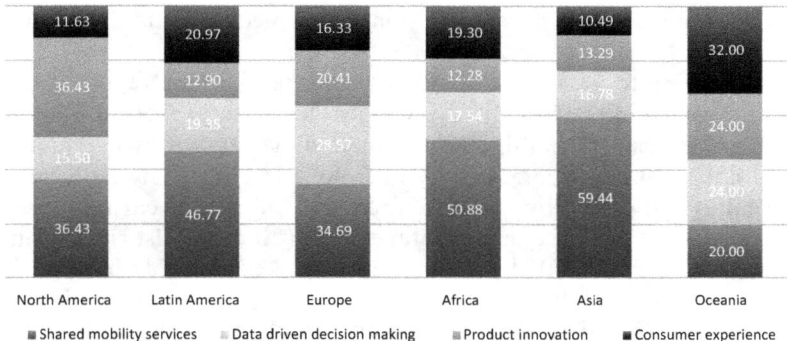

Figure 2.5 Start-ups financed worldwide (%)
Source: Canales et al., 2017 on Data Angel's List & CrunchBase 2016

The data in Table 2.1 shows how the sharing mobility sector excels in the ranking of the top ten of the most funded start-ups around the world. Among the 335 unicorn start-ups worldwide, ten are in the area of sharing mobility, representing 15% of the total cumulative value (almost $163 billion out of an overall $1,090 billion). Among the top ten, we find three of these start-ups: in second place sits the American-owned Uber and, in the third, the Chinese-owned Dixi Chuxing, followed by the Malaysian company, Grab Taxi, which sits in the tenth place. The data therefore shows that the most valuable sharing mobility services are in the US and Asian markets, rather than

Table 2.1 Top ten decacorn start-up

Rank	Name	Industry	Country	Valuation ($B)
1	Bytedance	Digital media/AI	China	75
2	Uber	Urban mobility	US	72
3	Dixi Chuxing	Urban mobility	China	56
4	WeWork	Facilities	US	47
5	Airbnb	Tourism	US	29.3
6	Stripe	Fintech	US	22.5
7	SpaceX	Transportation	US	18.5
8	JUUL Labs	Consumer electronics	US	15
9	Epic Games	Gaming	US	15
10	Grab Taxi	Urban mobility	Singapore	14

Source: www.cbinsights.com/research-unicorn-companies

in the European ones, and that they are predominately ridesharing services (8 on 10). To find a European start-up we have to go down to 154th place in the ranking where we find the French carpooling service, BlaBlaCar, which operates long- and medium-haul carpooling services.

According to data from the Digital Market Outlook report (2018), total revenue in the Mobility Services sector[4] was $329.561 million in 2016, of which 5.97% ($19.676 million) was generated by car rentals and about 10.17% ($33.528 million) from ridesharing. By 2018, total revenues had grown by about 27%, during which time car rental services had lost almost one percentage point (5.06%) whilst ridesharing had grown significantly by 14.26%. It is expected that ridesharing will continue to rise to almost 19% by 2020. Globally, China currently falls behind the US and Europe in terms of its contribution towards global revenues of Mobility Services ($67.0 billion compared to $117.6 billion in the US and $102.8 billion in Europe, of which $22.0 billion is generated in the UK alone), but it has the highest forecast for growth by 2022, when it is expected to account for approximately +13.8% of revenues, compared to the US (+5.7%) and Europe (+8.1%).

Between 2016 and 2018, the number of car rental (including car sharing) users increased, however ridesharing numbers grew far more substantially during this time. Car rental users grew from almost 81 million to just under 87 million (an increase of +7% in two years), while ridesharing users grew from approximately 364 million in 2016 to almost 469 million in 2018 (an increase of +28.8%). According to several other estimates, vehicle-sharing systems represent the slowest and least dynamic area of growth in the sharing mobility sector. For example, it is expected that car sharing will represent only 10% of car rental fleets by 2020 (Merill-Lynch and Bank of America, 2018). Of the 197 operators active worldwide (Frost and Sullivan, 2016), 71% are active in Europe, and 14% are active in both Asia (38) and North America (38), respectively, while only 2.25% are represented in Latin America (6). However, the Asia-Pacific area accounts for about 38% of the global market, compared with 36% of the European market and 26% of the American market (Roland Berger, 2017).

Recently, Navigant Research (2018) analysed the global car-sharing market, examining its main benefits and market forecasts until 2024. It estimates that global revenues from car-sharing services will grow from $1.1 billion in 2015 to $6.5 billion in 2024, with the Asian market once again expected to record the highest percentages in growth during this time. In China, for example, the car-sharing fleet was estimated at 14,000 vehicles. By 2016, this had nearly doubled to 26,000, with estimates suggesting that it will reach 100,000 vehicles by 2020 (an annual growth rate of +45%) (Roland Berger, 2017). Another interesting feature of China is that car-sharing services are managed entirely by local operators, which is very different to the European market in which large global automotive groups control a significantly greater market share. Of the 22 operators present in China, only 2 are global (Car2go and Car2share), but new groups like BMW and Volkswagen are about to enter. Moreover, according to a survey prepared by Lloyd's of London (2018), Chinese consumers are among the largest consumers of sharing services in the world (60%) compared with the US (47%) and the UK (47%), which represent the two other markets where the sharing economy is most developed. Cumulatively, this evidence suggests that the Chinese market for car-sharing mobility is one to watch over the next decade.

The data available on the diffusion of bike sharing worldwide also highlights the centrality of Asian markets, and in particular the Chinese market. According to the available data on the Bike Share Map,[5] the service is present in 406 cities around the world, with the largest number of bikes found predominantly in Asian cities: Suzhou e Wujian (24,422), Hángzhōu (23,794), Weifang (23,730), Taipei and Taoyua (22,033), Quanzhou and Luoj (14,610), Kunshan (11,691), Xuzhou (11,143), Paris (10,311), New York City (10,024), and London (9,788) rank significantly lower in the top ten rankings. The US is, however, where bike-sharing services have spread to the greatest number of cities (105). This is followed by China (61), Germany (40), Poland (37), and France (28). By contrast, Japan (4), India and South Korea (2) lag far behind the US and China in terms of urban bike-sharing services. At the same time, the vitality of the European market should be emphasised. Many European cities have developed ambitious plans for boosting cycle traffic in city centres. For example, Copenhagen is aiming for bike transport to make up 50% of inner-city traffic by 2025.

As already noted, ridesharing is the service that records the most significant future growth prospects in terms of revenues and users. As such, it is the service attracting the most attention from investors. According to the Digital Market Outlook (2018), China will continue to be the world leader for both revenue (approximately $29.749 billion) and for user penetration (20.9%) for the foreseeable future. This is expected to be followed by the US (17.8%), the UK (14.5%), Denmark (14.3%), and Finland (13.8%). In Europe, particularly in France and Italy, the ridesharing sector has come up against major resistance from taxi drivers that operate in a protected market. This circumstance has largely curbed the development of ridesharing, particularly automated ride-sourcing systems such as Uber. However, this has given some the opportunity to develop extra-urban carpooling systems, such as those developed by BlaBlaCar. Today, the BlaBlaCar community has over 35 million members in 22 countries (including three emerging markets in Turkey, India, and Mexico) and operates from 16 offices all over the world. Thanks to BlaBlaCar, France has become the most mature market for carpooling but there are other interesting carpooling initiatives elsewhere in Europe, like CHUMS,[6] which is a service that links together the five self-described "champion cities" of carpooling in Europe (Craiova – Romania, Edinburgh – the UK, Leuven – Belgium, Perugia – Italy, Toulouse – France) in order to "attract carpoolers, to keep the numbers rising and generate a core and profitable market for carpooling across Europe".

Despite these carpooling initiatives, it's clear that ride-sourcing and ridesharing services are experiencing the greatest expansion in the sharing mobility sector, and although there are examples of ridesharing platforms in Europe, such as Cabify in Spain, or the French Heetch, it is US companies Uber and Lyft that are the pioneers and leaders of e-hailing services around the world. At the time of writing, Uber continues to be a leader in terms of market value. However, new companies operating in emerging markets are attracting more capital. Ola, for example, was founded in India only two years after the arrival of Uber in 2013. It now exceeds the US company by market share (56.2% vs. 39.6%) and continues to grow after recently acquiring $2 billion of new funding. Moreover, Didi Chuxing is now second largest ridesharing company in terms of market value (approximately $56 billion) boasting over 50 million active users and more than 100 million rides a week. Thanks to the support of investors, Didi acquired Uber in China in 2016, forcing the US company to be an investor rather than an operator in the Chinese market.

In summary, we can say that sharing mobility seems to galvanise entrepreneurial energies and investors, especially in the field of ridesharing and in large urban areas, and especially in rapidly growing Asian economies. Fast growth in those areas is strongly correlated not only with population expansion in urban areas, but also with growing levels of internet connectivity and, as we saw earlier, a cultural acceptance of the sharing economy.

How sustainable is sharing mobility?

The data analysed in the previous section seems to support the notion that sharing mobility is the inevitable destiny of mobility. However, through careful examination of the data, we can only partially confirm the enthusiasm of investors and entrepreneurs. The current analysis of the future of mobility rarely focuses on understanding how sustainable the transition towards a sharing mobility system will be, and instead tends to focus on the economic potential of these services. In the following, we assess if there is a risk of an asymmetric transition for sharing mobility, in which economic sustainability is put before environmental or social sustainability.

Economic sustainability

Despite its expectations for economic growth, car-sharing services have failed to achieve much in the way of market penetration. For example, in Switzerland, where car sharing was born, less than 3% of license holders are car-sharing members, and the average occupancy rate for cars remains 1.56 persons (Swiss Federal Statistical Office, 2017). In Italy, where the service developed later than in the rest of Europe, no more than 2% of Italians with a license are car-sharing users (ONSM, 2016). In the municipality of Milan where there are five active car-sharing operators (Car2go, DriveNow, Guidami, Share'ngo and Enjoy), only 0.25% of trips in the city are done through car sharing. Research on Italian car sharing suggests that despite an annual growth rate of almost 16% at a national level, the five principal service providers in the country have losses of €27 million, amounting to €4,700 for each vehicle shared.[7] Users are increasing but not at a pace to guarantee a high level of profitability for the operators, which raises questions over their ability to survive. Added to this, there are high maintenance costs, costs to cover damage or misuse of vehicles, and fees that operators must pay to municipalities, which can vary between €300 and €1,200 per year for each vehicle. Car-sharing services continue to attract a niche of consumers who are lured by the opportunity of free subscriptions and sign-up bonuses. Many subscribe to more than one operator at the same time. Nevertheless, usage rates remain very low, with members often making less than one short distance trip a week (between 1 and 11 km). This has led some to suggest that car sharing is actually more profitable for the municipalities than it is for the service providers. The providers seem to bear these losses and consider them an investment of "research and development"; the logic being that the socio-economic transformations of sharing mobility over the long term will eventually lead to profitable businesses.

Even the American market of car sharing, now among the most profitable, has faced many difficulties. For instance, only 15 out of the 34 car-sharing programmes that emerged between 1997 and 2009 remain in operation today. That said, the impact of technology in the American case has led to positive improvements in the sector in the form of its usability, especially with regards to the transition from station-based systems to free floating systems (TCRP, 2016).

Bike-sharing services have also run into problems despite their growth over the past decade. The success of these schemes depends very much on the configuration of the cities in which they are developed (both in terms of morphology and cycling infrastructures) and on their cycling culture. For example, these services have been a great success in Chinese cities but not elsewhere. Even then the growth of bike sharing in China has not stopped some providers, like BlueGoGo and GoBee, from failing. In other areas we have seen similar exits. O Bike, a company from Singapore, declared bankruptcy in Germany, before auctioning more than 10,000 bicycles at €69 per piece. Scialpi (2018) suggests that these failures could be partly linked to the differences in bike-sharing culture between Asian and European countries.

The introduction of dockless, *free-floating bike-sharing systems*, has eliminated a management cost but it has also increased cases of theft and vandalism within the sector, which providers try to deal with through the provision of economic incentives. The French case of Vélib' in Paris is emblematic of this. Since the beginning of 2007, the service has represented a benchmark in Europe and has been imitated in cities such as London and Milan, reaching almost 290,000 subscribers. However, in recent years, subscriptions have fallen to 210,000 as the rate of damage to vehicles has exceeded 80% and incidents of vandalism and theft have risen. These factors have significantly reduced the number of users, lowered consumer satisfaction, and negatively affected the reputation of the service.[8] What is interesting is that despite their limited user base, the high costs of operation and the fact that they often run at a loss, bike-sharing schemes across the world are strongly supported in economic terms by the municipality, who want to promote and sustain such services. This is something not usually seen with other sharing mobility services such as car-sharing services.

Even ridesharing systems are not always successful despite their reasonable market performance in terms of user penetration, especially in the US and Asia. In many cases, it is a business that struggles to become fully profitable worldwide due to the strong tendency for market concentration and monopolisation. For example, America is one of the most developed ridesharing markets and yet Sidecar, a competitor of Uber and Lyft, shut down in December 2016 after attracting "only" $45 million in funding that year. By contrast Uber raised $12.5 billion and Lyft $1.8 billion in that same year, which gives us some indication of these market concentration tendencies and why Sidecar had to fold.[9] Even then, the market leaders still struggle to make a profit. In 2018, Uber generated almost $11.3 billion in net revenue worldwide. However, their latest financial report, submitted for their 2019 IPO, showed that the company has accrued a deficit of $7.9 billon, which leaves it significantly out of pocket. This perhaps explains why Uber's IPO on Wall Street has not gone well. Despite being one of the biggest stock market exchanges in history, Uber's opening share price of $42 was forced over three points below the fixed placement price at $45 on its opening day, leaving it to close with at a share price of $41.57 (a market value fall of 7.62% on its first day of trading). There are many reasons that might explain Uber's lack of profitability, including the limited success of some collateral services (i.e. Uber Eats or Uber Rush in the sharing delivery services), and huge legal expenses defending against workers, competitors, or partners, like in the lawsuit with Alphabet Inc.'s Waymo. Indeed, many of these losses are expected in Uber's current model of rapid expansion where the drive to build a large user base comes before anything else. That said, Uber has not been able to dominate in all markets. For example, it has now lost the Chinese market and is already being overtaken in the Indian market by operators such as Ola. Moreover, although the service has had great success in the US, the same thing cannot be said for the Europe, which is much more protected from the point of view of the labour market and transport regulations (see Chapter 4).

In research conducted in Italy, a process of optimisation and concentration of the market was identified, in which the biggest players were found to be the only ones who managed to survive successfully (Arcidiacono, 2018). There were numerous cases of bankruptcy for those not able to compete at the top level. In total, the study identified about 36 companies in the Italian market of sharing mobility, of which 40% were active in ridesharing and 60% were active in vehicle sharing (car and bike). Considering only ridesharing and peer-to-peer sharing, there was a collapse of these active platforms between 2016 and 2017, from 25 to 12. This is an effect partly generated by the difficulty of operating in this market, due to the growing hostility of traditional operators and the constraints of regulation that risk freezing-out investors and therefore the arrival of new companies. In addition, the hegemonic role played by the large global platform (i.e. BlaBlaCar) makes it very difficult for all other competitors to reach the same levels of success. However, because these large platforms attract the most attention from regulators, smaller companies have been able to grow in some cases. For example, the decision of the Italian labour court to prevent UberPOP from operating on the market was beneficial for new operators wanting to enter the market. Companies like Zego, a national start-up active in three cities (Milan, Turin, and Genoa), are evidence of this. Similarly, Heetch, a French start-up company operating in France, Belgium, and Sweden has been allowed to grow as Uber takes the heat of regulation in these markets.

In short, there are many uncertainties for the future development of sharing mobility. New services face strong competition and high-investment targets. This has led some to concentrate on the development of collaborations and joint ventures. For example, the Daimler and BMW group announced in April 2018 that they had formed a joint mobility company that combines their Car2go and DriveNow car-sharing services. The two brands will collaborate in different business areas related to the innovation of mobility services. They intend to focus on multimodal and on-demand mobility apps like Moovel and ReachNow, combine the services of Mytaxi, Chauffeur Prive, Clever Taxi, and Beat, and combine the parking services Park Now and Parkmobile Group/Parkmobile with ChargeNow and Digital Charging Solutions. The aim of this strategy led by the two leaders of the European car-sharing market is clear: they want to optimise and combine their efforts to make the most of a volatile market, where market competition and growth rates remain unstable.

Environmental sustainability

There are numerous studies that underline the positive impact of sharing mobility from an environmental point of view, although the significance of this impact varies widely amongst this research. Many of the studies conducted in the US (Cervero et al., 2003, 2006; Price et al., 2006) or in Europe (Haefeli et al., 2006; Maertins, 2006) have shown how station-based car rentals significantly reduce overall vehicular traffic (in terms of vkm). However, these reductions can vary significantly: from a 2% reduction, as shown in one of the first studies of San Francisco (Cervero et al., 2003), to a 45% reduction, as shown in a study of Bremen (Free Hanseatic City of Bremen, 2005). As for free-floating services, data collected (Martin and Shaheen, 2016; Martin et al., 2010) for several American and Canadian cities showed lower vehicle traffic reduction rates than observed in the station-based systems. For example, as a result of these schemes, traffic was said to be 6% lower in Calgary and 16% lower in the cities of Vancouver and Washington.

Successes and failures 35

A study of Montreal (Sioui et al., 2012) pointed out showed that among those who did not own a car, people who used car sharing were likely to drive more than those who did not use it. In the same way, among those who owned one or more cars, car-sharing users would tend to drive less than non-users. A study carried out in Italy (Arcidiacono and Pais, 2018) shows how user motivations related to sustainability were by far the lowest when compared to other motivations (see Figure 2.6). For these car-sharing consumers, only 7.9% were motivated by a desire for sustainable transport, while 46% were motivated by its flexibility, versatility, and freedom; and 38.5% were motivated by a greater freedom of transit in restricted traffic zones. Added to these are also motivations of exploration, driven by the desire to experiment with new forms of urban mobility (37%). Similar results also emerged in a study conducted in Germany about peer-to-peer car sharing, where it is very common among consumers (Wilhelms et al., 2016). By conducting a series of laddering interviews, this research revealed a hierarchical structure based on four motivational patterns: (1) economic interest, (2) convenience, (3) quality of life, and (4) certitude. Sustainability and environmental concerns were not recognised as key drivers, but rather were perceived as an indirect consequence of participating in car-sharing schemes.

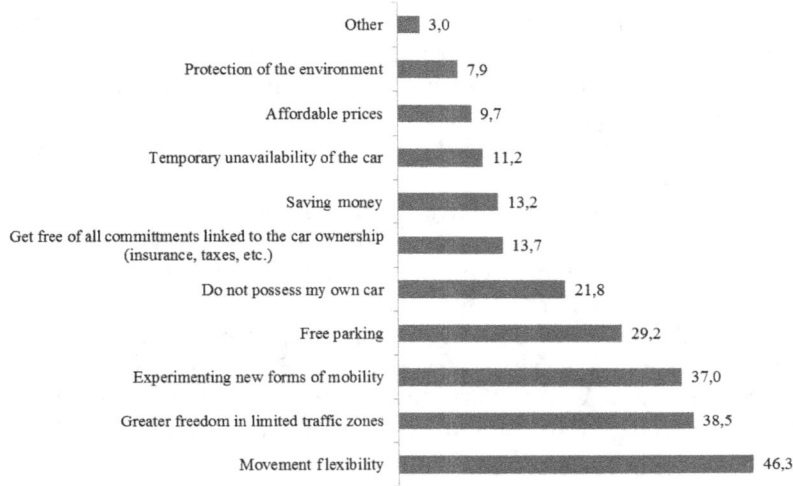

Figure 2.6 Reasons given for subscribing to the Car2go service (multiple choice %)
Source: Our elaboration on Car2go experience survey 2016

Different elements of analysis emerge in terms of environmental impact if we consider the so-called "inter-modality" of transport. A mobility survey of five North-American cities by Martin et al. (2016) revealed that there has been a 12% average reduction in the use of trains, 25% in the use of buses, and 55% in the use of taxis between 2014 and 2015. The study also found an average increase of 11% of journeys made on foot. Conversely, in the French context (Ademe, 2015a, 2015b), there has been a 25% increase in the use of urban rail transport. A survey carried out on the Car2go service found that 65% of users of the service were less likely to use taxis after the introduction of car sharing (Arcidiacono and Pais, 2018). At the same time, 48% of these users declared that if there was no option for car sharing, they would have used public transport (ibid.). Similar results are found in studies measuring the impact of bike-sharing services in the US and Europe (Ayuntamiento de Sevilla, 2010; Murphy and Usher, 2015). These studies highlight how bike sharing has a limited impact on substituting walking, private bicycle, and mass-transit services. This result is also confirmed by a study conducted in seven major cities (Hangzhou, Shanghai, Beijing, Paris, Barcelona, Lyon, and London) by Clean Air Asia (Mateo-Babiano, 2015). The study shows how before the introduction of the service, 42% of bike-sharing users used public transport, with only 10% previously using private transport. Things do not seem to change if we also consider ridesharing services. The Mass Transit Rider Research Report (2018) found that 65.4% of Uber and Lyft users had never used ridesharing services in conjunction with public transit, with only 21% stating that it happened infrequently. These results highlight how sharing mobility services have become competitors with traditional forms of transport, especially taxis and buses.

Sharing mobility, particularly station-based car-sharing services, is reducing the number of cars on the road, despite the fact that many of these services are based on the use of private automobiles, which continue to have environmental impacts. Early studies of car-sharing users conducted in the US (Cervero and Arrington, 2008; Lane, 2005) and Europe, particularly in Germany (Free Hanseatic City of Bremen, 2005; Rydén and Morin, 2005), Switzerland (Haefeli et al., 2006), and the UK (Myers, 2009) showed that approximately 20%–40% of cars were sold or scrapped following the adoption of a car-sharing service. Similarly, data provided by the TRSC research centre at the University of Berkeley (Stocker et al., 2016) on the use of the Zipcar service found that an estimated 20% of users were driving a car, and another 20% avoided buying a car or postponed a vehicle purchase. Studies elsewhere have recorded a similar impact, but to a lesser degree. A study of London (Carplus, 2015) found that 14% of users now avoided or postposed buying a car, whilst a study of five American cities where Car2go operates a free-floating car service found this reduction to be between 2% and 10% (Martin et al., 2016).

However, there are limitations to these findings due on the fact that they were based on what was declared by users, which tends to lead to overestimations, and because they neglect other contingent factors. For example, the economic crisis during the first of these studies on car-sharing could have influenced the statements made about giving up the car; a trend that would possibly be reduced in the post-crisis period, as evidenced by the recovery of the world car market. Furthermore, both structural and social factors, which concern the socio-symbolic relevance of the car as "good" (and consequently its desirability), the cultural factors linked to its use, as well as the contextual specificities in terms of quantity and quality of transport alternatives availability, can explain this strong variability in time and space.

From this point of view, the insights that come from the observation of the impact of sharing mobility in emerging markets such as China and India are interesting. In a Chinese study carried out using qualitative methodologies, it emerged that the greatest motivation for consumers using sharing services was the opportunity to travel in luxury cars (Zeng and Lane, 2015). Half of the respondents from this study said that they look at the car as a status symbol, which supports the notion that, in China, the car is a cultural symbol of achievement and prosperity. It is therefore perhaps not surprising that this study also highlights strong aspirations for vehicle ownership, which seems to coexist with the interest in car sharing. Nevertheless, if people's goal is to own a car for cultural reasons, this represents a barrier to the development of car sharing and will have further environmental impacts in terms of more polluting cars on the road. Another Chinese study (Hui et al., 2017), focusing on the behavioural patterns of active car sharing over a one-year period in Hangzhou, found that the number of long-term users increased by a ratio of 4.5%. Moreover, these long-term members considered car sharing as a substitute to private cars or public transport, which is different to what happens in Europe, where users are adopting car sharing as a complementary means of transport, for instance, to go shopping or to attend an event in their leisure time (Arcidiacono and Pais, 2018). Similar considerations can also be seen in India, where the success of ridesharing has actually increased the number of Indians wanting to own a car, and also begin working as a driver.[10]

Other studies of ridesharing and carpooling offer interesting results in terms of their environmental impact and effect on urban congestion. Analysis of London and Paris carried out by Inrix or Boston Consulting showed that there is no a positive correlation between the increasing use of ridesharing platforms and urban traffic congestion. Moreover, a study by the American Public Transport association showed that those routinely using a combination of several shared modes (such as ridesharing, car sharing and bike sharing) were more likely to take the metro or bus than use a private car (APTA, 2016). Conversely, in one study on the city of Boston led by the Metropolitan Area Planning Council (MAPC, 2018), and another conducted in Boston, Chicago, Los Angeles, New York, the San Francisco Bay Area, Seattle, and Washington, DC (Clewlow and Mishra, 2017), data suggested that ridesharing systems would likely increase congestion and urban pollution. The reason being that 60% of users for these studies said that were the option of ridesharing not available, they would use private rather than public transit.

In regard to carpooling, opposite trends are emerging. One study of French carpooling (CGDD, 2016) showed how these services increased the average number of car occupants by over 50%, from 1.4 passengers per vehicle to 3.5. Further studies of the French market by Ademe (2015a, 2015b) allow us to compare these effects between short- and long-distance forms of carpooling and to compare the differences between passengers and drivers. In the case of long-distance carpooling, 67% of members said they would prefer to use their own vehicle, 24% said they would use the train/TGV, 1% would opt for the bus or plane, and 8% wouldn't travel. The algebraic sum of the reductions of the journeys made by passenger and driver results in a decrease of 4% vehicle traffic, and each crew of carpooling involves a decrease of about 2 km of train journeys and 0.07 km by air, with a reduction of CO_2 emissions by around 12%. This data reveals how short-distance carpooling has an impact in terms of reducing vehicle traffic that is more significant than long-distance carpooling.

Moreover, many studies highlight how carpooling and mass transit journeys differ in their duration and cost. In some of the cities examined (such as Lille, Barcelona, and Frankfurt) we can see that a carpooling journey takes less time than a trip by bus or plane even if travelling on approximately the same route (factoring in the connection, embarkation, and disembarkation times). However, when high speed services are available, the train remains the fastest and cheapest way to travel, with journey times estimated to be between 20% and 70% quicker. A French study (Ademe, 2015a, 2015b) highlights how carpooling can increase inter-modality because the main pickup points of passengers are usually located at metro/bus/train stations, a factor that is also confirmed by an Italian survey of BlaBlaCar users (Arcidiacono et al., 2016). JoJob's (2016) study found that an Italian start-up focusing on corporate carpooling allowed members to measure the environmental impact of their journeys through their online service, which was then said to help increase car occupancy rates and reduce CO_2 emissions. Data collected from 2,000 company employees participating in the service suggests that 646,900.82 km of homework journeys were avoided, which amounts to over 105 tons of CO_2 and an average saving of €611 per employee.

Having now assessed the economic and environmental sustainability of the shared mobility paradigm, we must now move on to examine how these elements relate to its social impact. There is especially a need to analyse how sharing mobility is affecting the everyday practices of mobility, labour, and social life. In the following chapter, we turn to these issues; to discuss sharing mobility in the context of mobility justice and to examine how the future of urban mobility must take into consideration the collective rights we have to sharing mobility.

Notes

1 Although always with great differences, ranging from 60.2 years of Africa to 79.2 in North America and, in particular, in Europe there is the largest percentage of over 60 (25%).
2 This is not a general trend, and instead there are countries where the number of drivers is growing like Finland, Israel, the Netherlands, Switzerland, Spain, Latvia, Poland, China, India, and Brazil.
3 Look at www.autoexpress.co.uk/volvo/105286/this-is-not-a-car-show-volvo-plans-an-empty-stand-at-the-la-motor-show.
4 The data includes the various transport services: flights, car rentals, train and buses, ridesharing.
5 http://bikes.oobrien.com.
6 http://chums-carpooling.eu/it/.
7 www.quattroruote.it/news/mobilita_alternativa/2017/09/25/car_sharing_business_in_profondo_rosso.html.
8 www.theguardian.com/world/2018/may/04/paris-bike-share-scheme-velib-hi-tech-upgrade-problems.
9 See at: http://fortune.com/2018/02/14/uber-2017-financial-results/.
10 https://qz.com/india/1200878/with-uber-in-crisis-ola-zooms-ahead-in-indias-taxi-wars/.

3 Sharing mobility, mobility justice, and the right to the city

(Im)mobilities

Sophia no longer has a car; she gave it up years ago when she first moved to the city. It was too costly to keep a car that she rarely used. Besides, she found the experiences of driving in the city to be a stressful, time consuming and bad for the environment. For much of her everyday life, she now travels between home, work, friends and events using the public bus and metro service. These services are relatively cheap, conveniently located near her house and work, reasonably efficient and usually reliable, despite the occasional day of travel chaos caused by bad weather or overrunning engineering works. When she does need a car; for a weekend trip, to pick up her family's weekly grocery shop or on the rare occasions that she makes it to a party that goes on late into the night, she simply reaches for her smartphone and opens one of a number of shared mobility apps that were recommended to her by friends. She regularly uses one of these apps to book the conveniently located Zipcar nearby her house. On the occasions that she does end up at a party, she almost always books an Uber home to save herself from the drudgery of the meandering night bus.

Andrea, a migrant worker from Eastern Europe lives not too far from Sophia but has a very different experience of moving about the city. She works a great distance from her home, and it often takes her an hour and two buses to get there on a good day. Andrea is poorly paid for the job she does, and the income she does have is not enough to afford the metro to work. Sometimes she is forced into using it if the bus doesn't turn up or if she's running late. This is a decision not taken lightly as the extra cost will mean making sacrifices elsewhere in her tight weekly budget. She's seen and heard about some car-sharing services, has occasionally been in an Uber and has the app installed on her phone, but the reality is she cannot afford to use them save for a special occasion, nor does she have a driving license to try a car-sharing service or a full understanding of how they work.

These short vignettes are designed to highlight how everyday mobilities are not equal. As the cases of Sophia and Andrea suggest, freedom of movement is not a given, but instead is a complex issue influenced by a broad range of factors (Cresswell, 2010). It is now well recognised that movement of all kinds can be affected by intersecting factors including race, gender, sexuality, culture, access to capital, access to services and knowledge of how to use them, accessible infrastructures, safe routes of passage, social relations, and the various ways in which mobility is represented (Daconto, 2017; Jensen, 2009; Sheller and Urry, 2006). In short, these scholars ask that any analysis of mobility should take into account the fragmented politics, histories, and spatialities of society because it is these factors, and not simply transportation technology, that shape our experiences of mobility (Sheller, 2018). When new modes of transport, including sharing mobilities, are introduced, these factors are all too frequently ignored in favour of instrumentalist approaches based on technological rather than socio-technical solutions. To take but one example, ridesharing technology has had a significant impact on urban mobilities over the past decade, and yet it is not a service available to everyone. A growing body of research from both academics and policymakers continues to find that access to ridesharing can be determined by one's capital, culture, gender, race, body, and location (Andreotti et al., 2017; Rosenblat et al. 2016; Shaheen et al., 2017). In this chapter, we examine shared mobility through the lens of *mobility justice*, to ask if and how these modes of transport address the inequalities of (im)mobility in the city (Sheller, 2018), or if and how they further entrench the free movement(s) of the kinetic elite whilst exacerbating existing inequalities subject to the mobile poor.

We address these questions by exploring and adapting the sociological concept of "the right to the city", which is the notion that cities should be spaces for all citizens to engage equally and collectively in practices pertaining to freedom of speech, movement, and access to a decent life in the city. In particular, we question our right(s) to sharing mobility in the city. We will look closely at the underlying values and practices of shared mobility to show where they merge, intersect, and diverge from the principles of the right to the city. As we saw in the previous chapters, the concept of sharing mobility does appear to exhibit ideals of the right to the city and of open access, community building, sustainability, and socially just mobile practices. However, it is time we asked: but at what cost and for whom are these ideals adopted and practiced for?

Following a discussion on what the principles of the right to the city mean in the context of sharing mobility, this chapter offers a critical discussion on the contradictory practices of car-sharing mobility. We demonstrate how, on the one hand, this rapidly growing industry positions itself as a socially and environmentally responsible solution to urban mobility, and on the other hand, (re)produces mobility injustices in cities all over the world. In drawing together these examples, the chapter aims to highlight the relations, tensions, and contradictions that emerge as the ideals and practices of sharing mobility are put into contention with our right to the city. Ultimately, we use this chapter to emphasise a relational approach to sharing mobility that focuses on the wide-ranging factors that influence one's right to contemporary sharing mobility. It is these relational factors, we argue, that need further consideration if we are to realise the potential of a culture of sharing mobility, which has benefits to cities, citizens, and the wider environment.

The right to sharing mobility

"The right to the city" can be defined as a philosophy and a collective right for urban inhabitants to have a meaningful influence, free from state or corporate interests, in the decisions and processes that shape the public spaces and practices of their lives (Harvey, 2013; Mitchell, 2003). This notion, made famous by the work of Henri Lefebvre (1968), offers a pathway for challenging the power of top-down urban governance by putting collective interests at the heart of decisions made about urban life. In recent years, the notion has been especially valuable for activists coordinating organised responses to wealth inequalities and democracy in the city (e.g. the Occupy Movement) and for community groups fighting the social and cultural effects of urban (re)development.[1] In reference to the sharing economy, it has been useful as a way to frame responses to the localised effects of urban "gig" work, short-term rentals, and surveillance practices (Shaw and Graham, 2017). Elements of this philosophy and practice can also be seen elsewhere, in the concept of the sharing city (McLaren and Aygeman, 2015; Shareable, 2018) and the sustainable city (Chatterton, 2018) where emphasis is placed on creating an urban way of living that is equitable and environmentally conscious. These concepts have been especially useful for developing ideas around how we might use technologies to achieve these goals, whilst avoiding the pitfalls of the popular smart city narrative, which has been criticised for reinforcing forms of top-down urban governance (Kitchin and Perng, 2016; Söderström and Klauser, 2014).

Largely missing from these debates is how urban mobilities are linked to the right to the city framework (Verlinghieria and Venturini, 2018).

The focus instead has been on the places in which we might fight for our right to the city; namely public spaces including squares, plazas, and streets. Shared mobility, key to many contemporary forms of urban mobility, has received even less attention in this respect despite the impacts it is having on everyday life in the city. In response to the growth and popularity of shared mobility, we suggest that the right to the city should not be considered static, as something only to be studied and fought for in specific locations. Instead, echoing Middleton (2018), we argue that the right to the city must also be studied and fought for in and through our everyday mobilities, which increasingly unfold through a spectrum of shared mobile practices. Questions of urban inequality and the right to civic spaces, discussion, and representation are not restricted to specific locations but instead are multifariously distributed about the city, including through its patterns and practices of mobility. In particular, we are interested in *who* has the right to sharing mobility in the city and *where* those rights can and cannot be exercised through different forms of shared mobility.

Building on Harvey's (2013) assertions that Lefebvre's original conceptualisation must be updated and adapted to suit the needs of the time, we suggest that the right to the city is a processual concept that demands to be rethought and reworked to reflect the always shifting context(s) of urban space. Lefebvre's Paris of 1968 is after all, markedly different to that of today. As documented in the previous chapter, cities around the world are currently undergoing immense changes in terms of population size, demographics, and socio-economic divides. This brings many new challenges to how we might conceptualise and practice our right to the city. How the principles of the right to the city can be adapted to fight for mobility justice is just one area for consideration amongst these changes. Nevertheless, we acknowledge that the right to the city is not without flaws, especially when we consider how these rights can quickly become distorted (Attoh, 2011). Lefebvre's rights can be ambiguous and difficult to pin down in practical terms. For instance, we could just as easily approach rights as socio-economic as we could as legal, moral, democratic, libertarian, individual, or collective. This leaves the right to the city paradigm with a problem of ambiguity over its definition, which must be addressed if we are going to continuously use the term to push for pragmatic changes in our cities. This is an issue when we address the question of *what rights for who?* Therefore, in order to make our position clear, we are concerned with the rights for affordable, safe, culturally sensitive, and sustainable mobilities for all city dwellers, especially for those currently underrepresented or exploited in the shared mobility economy. We understand these rights as relationally contingent rather than fixed, which is to say that these rights will have different meanings to different people, and we acknowledge the difficulties in advocating for and protecting these rights across the diversity of urban populations. However, if cities are to continue adopting shared mobility strategies, we argue that it is necessary to work through these difficulties if we want to develop livable cities for all.

Pseudo-sharing and the car-sharing market

Cities and their citizens have long embraced ideas of sharing mobility. This can be seen through the history of public transport and the welfare state, as well as through the history of formal and informal vehicle- and ticket-sharing schemes, where there has been an emphasis on sharing the spaces, practices, and costs of mobility. Much of this lives on. Public transit networks still exist today, and they do still encourage these principles to some degree, despite the increasingly fractured ways in which cost and access to them are splintered along socio-economic lines (Graham, 2001; Lucas et al., 2016). There should also be some recognition that the ideals of shared mobility are far better adhered to in large urban centres than elsewhere such as in rural areas, where high costs, inadequate accessibility, and increasingly poor networked connectivity have been said to create physical and digital divides. In the UK, a report by Lucas (2012) showed that rural transport exclusion has been recognised by transport planners, academics, and policy initiatives in recent years, however she also found that much of this discourse has not yet been translated into effective practice by transport providers. This suggests that there is a long way to go to eradicate what's known as "transport poverty" in rural areas.

Despite the rich history and urban-centricity of shared public transport services, in recent years urban centres have embraced novel forms of what Belk (2014) calls "pseudo-sharing mobility", where the intentions to profit from the movement of people are (poorly) concealed by the marketisation of narratives around "community" and "sharing". In the past ten years, urban mobility has been increasingly characterised by a swath of digital services that seek to disrupt and augment conventional mobilities by intentionally flooding markets in the hope of retaining users and their data, which are intended to be used for monetisation. Whether intentionally or not, these novel forms of shared mobility can effectively permit more freedom of movement to the mobile elite and further restrict the movements of the mobile poor. Indeed, pseudo-sharing mobility presents difficult challenges for the right to the city model because it suggests issues of urban mobility can be solved by market-led solutions and technological fixes. It is a model of shared mobility that (re)produces socio-economic exclusivity rather than a model that seeks to tackle mobility justice (Sheller, 2018). At a time when governments across the world are increasingly looking to the private technology sector to solve issues of urban mobility,[2] and the private mobility sector are increasingly looking to compete with public transportation services directly,[3] this leaves us with the serious challenge of how to make shared mobility a more socially just at the same time as making it attractive to the market. In the following, we highlight just some of the areas where the impacts of pseudo-sharing can be seen in the practices and attitudes towards sharing mobility.

Car-sharing services promise sustainable, socially responsible, and technological solutions to the issues of congestion, pollution, and individualistic-driving behaviours. Despite these promises, we might question whether car-sharing adopts the principles of sharing or the right to the city to any great extent, especially when we examine where these services operate, who they are available to, how technology mediates the experience, and what motivates people to take part. The goal of commercial sharing services, by far the largest in this market, is geared towards improving the efficiency and environmental impacts of transporting people. Whilst this is laudable and does have some positive impact such as bringing car ownership, travel costs, and CO_2 emissions down (Baptista et al, 2014; Nijland and Meerkewk, 2017; Shaheen et al., 2016; Viechnicki et al., 2015), we suggest these schemes are largely based on a for-profit model of market exclusivity that undermines much of these effects. Simply put, they are market solutions for those that have access to them, can afford them and have the knowledge of how to use them, rather than initiatives based on a model of social inclusivity or community building (a topic that we return to in Chapter 5).

This is clearly seen when we examine the geographies of stationary car sharing. For example, when we look at where Zipcars are located in London, we find that these locations map uneasily well onto areas of the city with higher socio-economic characteristics. This can be done by comparing Zipcar locations on the "Find Zipcars near you" tool on the Zipcar website with mapped socio-economic census data from the DataShine project.[4] As these maps of London show, Zipcars are more likely to be located in areas with affluent and highly educated professional occupants. If we focus specifically on Zipcar locations in East London, we can see that residents of Newham, a borough characterised by low levels of education and professional occupants (2011 census), cannot be said to have the same or even similar levels of access to Zipcars compared with boroughs to the west, which have higher levels of education and professional occupants. To make matters worse, a recent report on car sharing in London, commissioned by Zipcar, indicated future growth areas for membership that exclude areas with less attractive socio-economic characteristics (see Briggs, 2014). Despite the marketing messages that suggest otherwise, including the taglines "Wheels when you want them" and "Available 24/7, from convenient locations near where you live and work",[5] the result is that the distribution of Zipcars in London has a skewed geography, where access is denied by both geographical and socio-economic factors for large swaths of the population. This leaves the named benefits of this car-sharing service to be owned and enjoyed by a select group. It may well be the case that the market for stationary car sharing is deemed smaller for areas of the city with higher levels of car ownership (Briggs, 2014), but this does not mean that the introduction of such schemes will not help to encourage practices of car-sharing and reduce car ownership overtime. For a market in search of profitability, it is perhaps unsurprising that the main target is high spending consumers with sufficient financial resources and intensive mobility needs. Commercial car-sharing services are ultimately designed to attract these people, many of which live or work in the central areas of cities. Nevertheless, by doing so these services are limiting the opportunities for wider populations to participate in stationary car-sharing cultures. This begs the question of why these services have not been readily introduced as public services.

The (re)production of mobility injustices and the social inequalities of shared mobility identified here are echoed across the sector as well as in the literature. For example, evidence is emerging that suggests ridesharing services exclude areas deemed to be less profitable, which tends to be historically poor and racially diverse areas of the city (Ge et al. 2016). The effect is that these services are concentrated where the money is instead of being universally inclusive or accessible. Studies of stationary bike-sharing schemes have also shown similar patterns of uneven distribution, where parking docks are more likely to be found in affluent areas of the city (Clark and Curl, 2016; Gavin et al., 2016). Shaheen et al.'s (2017) study of the US market showed how social geographies, digital payment systems, lack of culturally inclusive marketing, and language barriers were all factors in why commercial services have uneven geographies of participation. This is further complicated in Andreotti et al.'s (2017) report on participation in the sharing economy, where they explicitly state the need to focus on understanding the many forms of digital participation divides that exist in this area. It is not enough, they argue, to say that a digital divide exists. Instead, they suggest that more must be done to understand the context of participation divides, which are socially, economically, and geographically contingent. We would add to this how the clear urban-centricity of the most prominent shared mobility services creates participation divides. Even when services have been introduced in rural areas (e.g. Uber in the US), participation rates have been comparatively low owing to the effects of insufficient service coverage, poor or intermittent cellular connectivity, a less digitally literate population, and that more people own or rent their vehicles in these areas (Shaheen et al., 2017).[6]

Representations of mobility also play a role here. Participation divides can be produced through representational practices that shape the meanings and experiences we associate with mobile practices (Nikolaeva et al., 2019). Thus, if one cannot see elements of themselves and their lifestyle in shared mobility marketing and discourse, then they might be less inclined to think that it is a service for them. Even a cursory look at the marketing imagery for shared mobility services reveals that they are not aimed at everyone. If shared mobility services and policymakers are interested in producing truly revolutionary changes to transport, they would do well to take these contextual and representational factors into account before delivering new services to market. By ignoring the complexities of mobility, the divides between the kinetic elite and mobile poor are likely to be further entrenched.

When we look at the factors that characterise the people using these services, we can begin to see who is attracted to these services and in what context, which again suggests that car-sharing mobilities are not evenly adopted around the world. Arcidiacono (2017), for example, identified and compared the user profiles of two shared mobility services in his study of 3,706 car-sharing users and 641 carpooling users in Italy. The resulting profiles highlight that users are likely to have similar educational levels, employment status, age, and gender.

- The smart worker (46.4%): mostly men in employment aged between 26 and 45 who discovered these services through the internet. These non-intensive users like to experiment with new ways of moving like car sharing, but disdain from forms of collaborative mobility such as carpooling.
- The flexible moving family (26.9%): typically, these users are self-employed workers, aged over 46, married and have families with more than 4 members. These users adopt this service for its flexibility, versatility, and convenience. They have come to know the service through the press but are not considered intensive users of the service.

- The city user (26.7%): primarily made up of people under 25, often university students and graduates, some of whom live in a family or share a home with peers and/or work colleagues. These users value the fun and convenience of these services. They are intensive users, signing up for rides at least once a week.

In the case of carpooling, two user profiles were identified:

- Experienced Travellers (45.1%): predominantly highly educated men with more than 20 trips in the last six months, who use the platform as drivers.
- Young Explorers (54.9%): predominantly young men with less than 20 trips in the last 6 months, who use the platform to save money on travel.

These findings are also echoed elsewhere in the literature focused on European and US cases. For instance, Schaller's (2018) study of ridesharing across the US found that those involved in these services were twice and even three times as likely to be aged 25–34, have a bachelor's degree, and earn over $50,000 a year (see also Kopp et al., 2015; Observatorie de la Confiance, 2014; Owyang, 2014; Stokes et al., 2014). In other contexts, for example, in Asia, we see different attitudes towards car sharing based on different cultures of car ownership. Research by Lane et al. (2015) suggests that car-sharing practices in this region are influenced by the social status that comes with owning a car. Whilst car-sharing services are increasing exponentially in this region, car ownership remains a key material measure of social mobility that complicates any universal picture that users are young, educated, and affluent. This highlights a key economic and cultural difference between those users likely to adopt car sharing in Europe and the US, where the social status of car ownership is seen to be declining, and those likely to adopt car sharing in Asia. It is also an area where further research is needed to understand how material cultures are interacting with the rise of shared mobility services.

The literature focused on the motivations for using car-sharing mobility services has also raised questions about how engaged the majority of people are with issues of sustainability and cultures of sharing. For example, Arcidiacono and Pais (2018) found that only 8% of users cited environmental factors as a reason for using Car2go in Milan, despite this being one of the primary selling points. There is a sense from this study and others (see Shaheen et al. 2016) that car sharing is a way for companies and users to meet their corporate and social responsibility without ever really questioning the underlying impacts of their practices, which are almost always economically driven. This is echoed in the broader literature on user motivations for the sharing economy, where financial motives rank higher than environmental sustainability motives for participation (Böker and Meelen, 2017; Schaefers, 2013). From these studies, we might then suggest that said consumer attitudes towards environmental sustainability do not always reflect the realities of the true reasons for embracing shared mobility, which tend to be predominantly economic. Nevertheless, as we highlight across this book, there are other cultural benefits to car sharing that we must consider, including participation in meaningful community practices.

Alongside these socio-economic characteristics, research into how those less able-bodied have used these services suggests that some services have little consideration for true inclusivity when we consider the spectrum of human bodies.[7] NYLPI's (2018) study of Lyft and Uber in New York, for example, found that long waiting times and a lack of adequately equipped vehicles (26% across the total combined fleets) remained significant barriers to entry for less able-bodied. This is despite the introduction of wheelchair accessible vehicles for Uber and Lyft, which were brought in to solve this issue. For wheelchair users especially, the NYLPI suggest this has effectively ruled out the use of these services for most everyday practices.

Finally, research on the security of car-sharing services has raised some questions about who is safe and insured, and how safety is enforced throughout car-sharing journeys. Cao (2016), for example, points out that Uber operates a ride-at-your-own-risk policy for both passengers and drivers, which we argue completely contradicts cultural notions of sharing. This is important because it shows how both drivers and passengers can be affected by issues of security, which highlights how the right to safe forms of shared mobility is not only an issue for passengers. It also reemphasises the platform model, which limits the responsibility that service providers have to ensure these interactions are safe. Cumulatively, these studies raise serious questions over who these services are really for, and serious doubts that they offer a right to sharing mobility in the city, despite the marketing assertions of these services that promote inclusive and sustainable transport solutions for urban citizens.

Towards inclusive sharing mobility

The right to the city is an ongoing battle. As Harvey (2013) suggests, we are still "charting the path" to create cities that are inclusive and functional. Sharing mobilities are a significant part of the necessary groundwork needed to achieve this goal. Contemporary shared mobilities are not set in stone, but rather subject to changes that we can all enact as part of our daily lives. Indeed, we believe there is great potential in sharing mobility that we could all benefit from. Shared mobility services are not going away, however, change will need to come quickly if the future of sharing mobility is not to be subsumed by profit-driven pseudo-sharing models that appeal to our economic sensibilities first and our social and environmental sensibilities second. This is particularly the case regarding car-sharing mobilities, which lead the market in many respects.

Following Douglass and Friedmann (1997), there is a need to reinvigorate participation in urban civil societies, which we argue includes a rethinking of our shared urban mobilities. At our current juncture, we believe the market vision of sharing mobility is a step away rather than towards the potential of sharing mobility. As we have demonstrated, the current technocratic approaches to sharing mobilities only work for a small minority. The evidence suggests that the majority of these services are not socially responsible, nor are they especially environmentally sustainable, despite their marketing messages. On the contrary, many such approaches have further encouraged individualised mobilities, exacerbated social inequalities, and resulted in a rise in traffic and emissions in our cities.[8] This is especially pressing when we consider the recent stark warnings from the IPCC (2018) that failure to act on reducing CO_2 emissions now will result in catastrophic impacts in the near future.

Alternative and not-for-profit approaches must be sought out by people, planners, city councils, and industry. The pertinent issues and impacts of contemporary mobility will not be solved by new technologies, infrastructure, and modes of transport alone. This does not mean moving away from technology, far from it, but it does mean changing the rationale for why and how technology is being developed and used. A focus on *who* these services are for needs to remain at the forefront of these efforts. Questions remain over how "disrupting" existing services to create "frictionless" experiences is of any significant benefit, especially if those services then fail to disrupt the status quo of urban shared mobility, which is based on a form of market individualism augmented by technology.

To make the most of shared mobility, and steer it in a different direction, we must explore new ways that these practices can be socially and environmentally just mobilities. The projects highlighted by the Shareable organisation (2018), including the SafeMoto motorbike sharing scheme in Kigali, the COOP taxi scheme in Seoul and the RideAustin ridesharing service in Austin are all examples of where this work has already begun. Although these cases can be difficult to scale, especially in large urban centres built around a culture of car ownership and individual consumerist practices, this should not stop us pursuing similar initiatives, which are necessary for significant change (see Chatterton, 2018). Following McLaren and Agyeman (2015) and more recently Katrini (2018) and Nikolaeva et al. (2019), we should shift our focus to developing urban sharing cultures and the commoning of mobility, which will help to distance cultural ideals of sharing from economic models of sharing. Doing so would help to develop localised and networked socialities from which shared mobilities could be organised rather than mobile practices mediated by technology platforms with little interest in community development. It is only by pursuing these changes that the collective right to sharing mobility can be realised.

However, this will require significant effort and financial support from city governments and citizens, where a major cultural shift is needed. This will not be easy at any level, but we are beginning to see these shifts, which does give us some indication as to how attitudes towards pseudo-sharing are changing. The recent #DeleteUber campaign is an example of this, as are the many cases where Uber is being challenged through the courts across the world on issues pertaining to employment practices, which we will discuss in the next chapter. Co-operative car-sharing services are also developing exemplary models, by offering users a stake in a social enterprise rather than a profit-driven scheme. Co-wheels, for example, is a co-operative that leads the way on wheelchair accessible car fleets and has committed to using electric vehicles wherever possible. They have worked with government departments in Scotland to develop car-sharing schemes supported by the tax payer, which prove that these cultural shifts can take place.

Ultimately, the right to sharing mobility is an issue of mobility justice and not simply an issue of transport. We argue that the right to sharing mobility should encompass more than simply access to public transportation. The right to sharing mobility must be socially, materially, and environmentally conscious, which means taking into account the relations between these factors. Shared mobilities, and any right we have to them, are always enmeshed with the movement of people, goods, services, culture, and information, and increasingly tied to climatic movements that both affect and are affected by these mobilities (Sheller, 2018). We therefore situate sharing mobility as localised spatial practices, but which are directly and intricately related to regional, national, and global spatial practices. Further attention is needed to join these dots, by those studying these systems of mobility, by those designing these systems, by those regulating these systems, and by those using these systems.

Notes

1 Nevertheless, as Attoh (2011) and Uitermark et al. (2012) have suggested, the right to the city initially proposed by Lefebvre does have a tendency to be distorted and misused in academic and media accounts of these social movements.
2 See for example the case of Innisfil, Canada, where the local authority has turned to subsidising Uber rides in leu of a public transit system. As Bliss (2019) shows, this effectively means that Uber controls the pricing of public transit and maintains ownership of mobility data for the area.
3 Uber's recent IPO documentation (April 11th 2019) shows clearly the companies' intentions to compete directly with public transportation companies (see www.sec.gov/Archives/edgar/data/1543151/000119312519103850/d647752ds1.htm#toc647752_7).
4 www.zipcar.com/en-gb/car-hire-london and http://datashine.org.uk/#table=QS803EW&col=QS803EW0003&ramp=YlOrRd&layers=BTTT&zoom=12&lon=-0.1500&lat=51.5200.
5 www.zipcar.com (2019).
6 This is an area of sharing mobility that needs further research, especially as service providers begin to trial rural services across the world.
7 To date there have been very few studies of the effects of shared mobility on less-able bodied mobilities. This is an area which needs significant attention in the future.
8 See for example, the case of Uber and New York, where traffic and emissions have become worse as a result of many more cars on the road (Schaller, 2018). Interestingly, it is New York authorities which are at the current forefront of attempts to regulate ridesharing in the city (see Chapter 4).

4 Regulation, platform governance, and the labour practices of shared urban mobility

The fragmented landscape of regulation

Shared mobility platforms are coming under increased scrutiny over the treatment and status of workers, their environmental impacts, and the socio-economic inequalities that they produce. There is a growing argument for developing effective regulatory frameworks that address these issues. At the same time, there is a growing resistance to the top-down and often rigid regulation of shared mobility by the state and local authorities, which are said to stifle competition and innovation in the sector, and a move towards iterative models of self-regulation and shared regulation, which are said to be better suited to the dynamism of the sector. Witt et al. (2015) have recognised this tension across the sharing economy, suggesting it is the current symbolic battleground for the long-standing political divides between the neoliberal free-market practices of (technology) companies and the role of the state in consumer practices. These deep-seated divides make it a challenging environment for both shared mobility platforms to operate and for regulators to introduce effective regulation.

How to accommodate and manage the impacts of shared mobility is a question on the minds of city authorities as it is in the minds of national and international policymakers, and those that work in this sector. Recently, we have begun to see authorities reacting to shared mobility, and particularly ridesharing services, based largely on the rhetoric of what regulatory measures can be implemented to ensure fair competition, suitable labour status, passenger safety, and sustainability. Examples of this can be seen across the world in the cities such as Barcelona, Cairo, Delhi, London, New York, Paris, and Sao Paulo, where regulations and temporary restrictions on ridesharing have been imposed over the last decade. Most recently, the City of New York, which we will show has become a test bed for regulation on ridesharing in recent years, suspended any new ridesharing licences entering the market for a period 12 months and introduced a minimum wage for drivers (from August 2018). This is an attempt to assess the impact that these services have on the existing taxi market, labour practices, and congestion within the city.[1] On a national level, Denmark, Bulgaria, and Hungary have all banned ridesharing as they attempt to understand the impact that these services are having on existing taxi markets, road congestion, air quality, and passenger safety. In other countries, for example in Poland and the UK, legislation that places ridesharing within the same regulatory framework as conventional taxi operations is the subject of ongoing debate amongst national and local authorities. In these cases, authorities are working towards common regulatory frameworks that mean ridesharing drivers and traditional taxi drivers must abide by the same rules around licensing, payment, and zoning.

Whilst ridesharing has been the focus of regulatory efforts, bike-sharing and scooter-sharing schemes have also begun to be targeted by regulators seeking to impose sanctions whilst they get to grips with how these practices are impacting on urban mobilities and the streetscape. One of the main concerns in this area is passenger safety and littering. City authorities in Auckland and Dunedin, for example, have placed temporary suspensions on the scooter service, Lime, after reports of technical malfunctions that resulted in serious accidents (Ainge Roy, 2019). Moreover, the Land Transport Authority in Singapore recently introduced fines and bans for free-floating bike-share users who fail to drop off bikes at designated public cycling park spaces.

Regulatory moves such as these have been hailed both as a step in the right direction and as an attack on innovation in the sector. We agree that these measures have been useful in curbing the disruptive power of global shared mobility platforms, but also that the rhetoric on which they have been based draws attention away from the wider issues of shared mobility (in)justice. We therefore use this chapter to call for regulation that tackles the interconnected issues of mobility justice, including transport equity and inclusion equality, environmental sustainability, labour precarity, health and safety, data privacy, and algorithmic transparency (Sheller, 2018). We do not see many of the current trends in regulatory practices doing much to address these issues. Instead, what we see are single focus regulatory practices adopted or adapted from transportation regulation that attempt to offer temporary fixes to a constantly shifting sector. As we argued in Chapter 3, sharing mobility has the capacity to be far more than a transportation sector; it has the capacity to be culture of practice that ensures mobility is a socially just and environmentally sustainable right for all people.

In this chapter, we argue against the notion that regulation in the sector will impede innovation and progress in the shared mobility sector. As McLaren and Agyeman (2015) and the Shareable organisation (2018) have shown, there are now many examples of effective regulatory measures that can address issues of mobility justice without limiting innovation. The notion that innovation and progress is prevented by regulatory measures is defined in terms that suit the sector's dominant platform model, which is largely innovation measured by economic growth driven by technological solutions for transport. It is innovation as defined by capitalism. As we argued in Chapter 3, this economic model of progress is ill-equipped to deal with issues of mobility justice, which are characterised by far wider social and environmental definitions of progress.

We suggest a different regulatory approach that seeks to respond to the relational impacts of shared mobility. By this we mean designing regulation that seeks to respond to socio-economic issues at the same time as it responds to environmental issues, urban congestion, accessibility, and fair competition. Consider, for example, regulation that would tackle the employment status of ridesharing drivers at the same time as that which hopes to reduce CO_2 emissions and congestion; or regulation that takes aim at ensuring services are accessible and inclusive inasmuch as they are affordable and sustainable. We suggest that responding to the relational impacts of shared mobility, regulatory authorities, and policymakers can begin to produce conditions that tackle issues of mobility injustice and realise the potential of sharing mobility. Without these changes, we believe that the promise of sharing mobility will remain only in a small number of localised services, leaving a much larger group of services to continue down a path that nullifies this potential.

In order to justify this approach, we must first outline the current state of regulation in the sector to highlight why there needs to be significant shifts towards models that respond to the issues of mobility (in)justice. The chapter is therefore split into the following six sections to account for the many factors that make up the topic of governing shared mobility. Even then, we can only claim to paint limited picture of the fragmented regulatory landscape that is emerging. First, we discuss how the perennial problem of defining shared mobility has a direct impact on how authorities regulate the sector. How this sector is segmented and defined has a significant effect on how regulators are responding to it, which we'll argue is a particular problem for a sector that is always evolving. Second, we discuss the practices and challenges of regulating shared mobility platforms; the aim being to illustrate the difficulties city authorities have when regulating global services in local contexts. Third, we turn our attention on labour practices, which have been at the forefront of efforts to regulate the sector in recent years. Discussing a number of high-profile cases alongside ethnographic evidence of ridesharing drivers in London, we highlight how employment status, pay, and algorithmically determined working conditions have become a key battleground for campaigners, drivers, and regulators seeking to address the impacts of ridesharing on labour. Fourth, we draw attention to the regulatory concerns around data accountability, which has become significant in debates of regulation in the sector; as a resource in the lobbying of deregulation, as a means to regulate people working for and using these services, and as an issue that raises ethical concerns about data privacy and bias. The fifth section "Data regulation" outlines emerging models of regulation to highlight how regulation is being rethought by a range of different stakeholders. Specifically, we highlight the modes of self-regulation, shared regulation, and iterative regulation. Finally, we bring together these threads to justify the need for a different, decidedly radical approach to regulation in the sector, which we call *relational regulation*.

The problem of terminology and effective regulation

As discussed in Chapter 2, the term "shared mobility" has been used to describe a diverse spectrum of mobility services, many of which have their own social, geographical, and historical contexts. This follows discussions of how to define the so-called "sharing economy", which is equally difficult when we begin to pick away at what we have meant by "sharing" at different times and places throughout history, and what we mean by "sharing" in different contemporary spaces (see Frenken and Schor, 2017). These contextual differences mean there can be no fixed or easy definition of shared mobility that can be used to regulate the sector. It is perhaps of little surprise then that there is currently no universal or systematic model or definition for regulating the sector across the world.

Part of the problem here is scale. The sector is made up of large global platforms inasmuch as it is by the small businesses and individual users that make use of these platforms to earn a living. Let's take the example of global ridesharing platform, Uber, and the local SafeMotos motorbike sharing scheme in Kigali, Rwanda to illustrate this. Both constitute ridesharing by offering the same fundamental service of connecting drivers with passengers looking for a ride through a digital platform. However, the two companies can hardly be said to be on the same playing field, with Uber's market value and international reach and impact far exceeding that of SafeMotos, which is locally bound to Kigali. To pursue and apply the same regulatory legislation for each of these services would be to nullify these significant differences. Equally, producing specific regulation for each individual ridesharing service, as is the current system, leads to the extremely fragmented regulatory landscape that we have today.

The historical, social, and political contexts of city transportation services have led policymakers to either produce their own categories of shared mobility or to draw services into existing categories of regulation. This means that regulatory measures are often different between countries, and even between cities in the same country. For example, In December 2017, the European Court of Justice ruled that ridesharing services were 'transportation services' rather than digital services. This opened up regulatory opportunities for EU states to apply existing transportation legislation (Bowcott, 2017). This contrasts with the US model, whereby ridesharing is currently categorised by each state, some of which have created a new category called "transportation network companies" (e.g. California and Virginia) to categorise ridesharing services for regulatory purposes. It also contrasts with the Ethiopian model, where the relatively closed national economic model determines that all transport businesses (including ridesharing services) are logistics companies, which must be owned and run by Ethiopians. In China, whilst there is a universal category of "online taxi booking business operations and services" to describe the work of ridesharing companies, it remains up to local authorities determine how to this sector is regulated (Zou, 2017).

The impact of this definition-by-jurisdiction approach has resulted in a regulatory landscape where different services are being compounded together without the consideration of differing scales, business models and motivations. As we will now demonstrate, regulating shared mobility has primarily become a practice of regulating platforms, especially ridesharing platforms. Whilst there are many good reasons for this, it does have implications for all services in the sector, many of which are not-for-profit platforms and yet get subjected to regulations as if they were.

The practices and challenges of regulating shared mobility platforms

Digital platforms thrive on what's called "network effects", which is the notion that the more networked users a platform has, the more successful it is in terms of generating profit and attracting investment capital (Srnicek, 2016). Network effects lead to monopolisation tendencies, whereby platforms with many users dominate markets and leave little room for alternatives. This can be seen with Uber in the same way as it can be seen with Google, with both holding what could be suggested is a near monopoly of ridesharing and search in some countries (e.g. US and UK). Network effects are generated and secured through enticing users onto the platform. With regards to ridesharing services, this is often done through enticing passengers through the free use of the app, relatively cheap costs of travel and sign-up bonuses, and through enticing new drivers through sign-up bonuses and marketed suggestions of a steady income. Key to the success of digital platforms is the data collected from these network effects. The more users a platform has, the more data it can collect and monetise, which usually happens through the packaging and selling of this data to advertisers and data brokers, or through the sale of data analysis expertise (Beer, 2018). Out of all the shared mobility platforms, Uber has arguably thrived the most from the network effects of its international user base, which is still growing at the time of writing. In return it continues to attract billions of dollars of venture capital investment based on the premise that the masses of data collected from users (meta data, behavioural data, locational data, financial data) will eventually be used to generate sustainable profits.[2] As ridesharing continues to grow in Asia, especially China, India, Indonesia, and Malaysia, where the largest market growth is expected, it will be interesting to see if Uber can maintain these network effects amongst rapidly growing services such as Didi, Go-Jek, Grab, and Ola, which rely on a similar model for growth.

As with other digital platforms, universal regulation of shared mobility platforms is incredibly difficult when we consider the geopolitical and historical landscape of national, regional, and local regulatory practices (Nooren et al., 2018), the different modes of service, and the sheer number of regulatory concerns that persist (market disruption, labour rights, the use of data and algorithms, health and safety, tax, insurance, traffic congestion, and environmental impact to name but a few). Effective regulation is made even more complicated by regulations that are contested, given as guidelines and not enshrined into law, and the fact that they are quickly outdated as the technology moves on (Sundararajan, 2016). Cumulatively, the topic of regulating shared mobility platforms is fraught with a myriad of complexities that are difficult to make sense of, let alone fully understand. The best we can do is offer specific examples of current practices, which we hope will act as a guide for future research to be done in this area. In light of this, the following will outline how regulators are responding to the challenges of market disruption, labour rights, data, and algorithms, which we see as key areas to focus on if we are to realise the potential of sharing mobility.

In the case of ridesharing platforms, regulatory authorities have, until relatively recently, been playing catch-up to the ways that these services flood city markets and affect mobility practices. The common practice has been for platforms to enter new markets either illegally or without prior warning, and then to seek forgiveness rather than permission from city authorities to continue operating. This follows the process of "creative destruction" made popular by Silicon Valley tech companies, whereby digital services seek to create and maintain capital growth through the continual disruption of existing markets.[3]

Lobbying has also become common place, with platforms employing professionals and tactics to game the system. Uber in New York, for example, lobbied support from users directly by highlighting what regulation would do to their experience. The creation of a "de Blasio button" was intentionally designed into the Uber app to show users how regulatory measures by the Mayor, Bill de Blasio would affect their wait times (Sundararajan, 2016). Regional and national authorities have also been lobbied with the help of expert lobbyists and ex-policymakers employed by platforms; the aim being to circumnavigate local regulatory conditions with the help of people that have influence and know regulatory systems work.[4] We can see these practices all over the world, from Delhi, London, and New York's regulatory battles with Uber, to Amsterdam's decision to remove dockless bikes from its streets.

In some cases, we are seeing tensions emerge between regulatory bodies. This was the case in Austin, Texas. Following a public referendum in 2016, the city introduced legislation requiring ridesharing drivers to provide their fingerprints for safety background checks to adhere to the policy for the existing taxi industry. This forced the non-compliant Uber and Lyft out of the city, which sparked a nation-wide row over the regulation of ridesharing in the US. Just over a year later, this legislation was overturned by the state of Texas, after millions of dollars has been spent by these companies lobbying for the ban to be lifted.[5] For the short period in between, Austin become a test ground for the kinds of shared mobility that favour a transport equity approach to ridesharing. RideAustin, a non-profit ridesharing app designed to pay a fair wage to drivers and keep costs low for riders was just one example of what filled the gap. The service offered an insight into what sharing mobility can be when supported by publicly backed regulatory measures. Since the return of Uber and Lyft to Austin, RideAustin has remained in operation but it is not yet clear if this model can compete with the artificially low pricing of the dominant platforms that are supported by venture capital.

Carpooling platforms, such as BlaBlaCar, have managed to avoid many of the regulatory battles fought by ridesharing platforms. This is largely because the model doesn't allow drivers to pick up ad hoc ride hailers or make any significant profit on their transactions with riders. In this sense it is not considered to be encroaching on existing taxi markets and therefore evades the regulatory measures imposed on services such as Uber and Lyft. This is despite the fact that BlaBlaCar still takes a cut from mediating transactions between drivers and riders in most of its operating markets. In the case of bike-sharing and scooter-sharing platforms, the problems are different. Littering, obstruction, maintenance, and damage to vehicles are seen as the issues for regulators to mitigate.

Labour rights and practices

It is now well known that the sharing economy has created novel forms and structures for labour practices and working environments (Schor and Attwood-Charles, 2017; Sundararajan, 2016). Any attempts to regulate shared mobility platforms have had to take these changes to labour into account, especially with regard to those services that have created the equivalent of full-time employment opportunities without the benefits of formalised employment. At the time of writing, there are many ongoing labour disputes between workers and sharing economy platforms fighting for their right to be recognised and treated as legitimate employees. So much so that labour disputes have become a significant battle ground for regulating sharing mobilities, and more widely in regard to the sharing and "gig" economy. In the following we focus on four of the most prominent aspects of these disputes, employment status, pay, driver/rider ratings, and "surge-pricing", though there are many other areas that we could consider.[6] We pay particular attention to Uber because it remains one of the most influential of services when it comes to labour rights and practices.

Ridesharing platforms are central to labour disputes because they have created conditions for full-time employment despite the claims that they operate as on-demand mobility services that offer flexible gig work. These platforms, led initially by Uber, simultaneously market themselves as providing a flexible working opportunity to raise some extra cash, whilst creating algorithmically manipulated conditions that operationalise user and driver data to influence driver behaviour and encourage more driving (Calo and Rosenblat, 2017; Rosenblat and Stark, 2016). It is indicative of Uber's knowledge that drivers do work full-time hours when the company responds to drive time regulations (such as those imposed by New York in 2018) by limiting drivers to a maximum of 10 hours "passenger time" within a 24-hour period and a maximum of 60 hours within a week (Uber, 2019). Were drivers to take full advantage of this over a week they would clearly be working in excess of the full-time hours expected by most employers. Moreover, as "passenger time" only counts for the time when a passenger is in the car, these stipulations do not account for driving to jobs or driving between jobs, which despite Uber's claims, is clearly part of the time spent working for Uber.

Uber has received the most attention from regulators with regards to the employment status of its drivers, which the company claims are self-employed contractors and not employees. To date, the employment status of Uber drivers has yet to be universally defined, with many cases still in the courts across the world. To give a flavour, Uber has been involved in disputes with drivers over labour status in Brazil, France, Spain, the UK, and some of the US states, where drivers have won the right to be recognised as employees rather than self-employed contractors. Uber has appealed or is appealing all of these decisions and has done very little to act on the consequences of these decisions, which have not yet been passed into law. In contrast to these cases, Australian courts have ruled that Uber can continue calling drivers self-employed contractors.

Whilst it has been found that most ridesharing drivers do not work the equivalent of full-time hours, it is also been found that a significant number do (Farrell et al., 2018). In the UK, for example, Uber claims that only 8% of its drivers work 60+ hours a week, which still amounts to 4,000 drivers.[7] However, this is complicated when we examine the practice of multi-app practices. For example, Rosenblat's (2018) study of New York ridesharing found that many drivers made up full-time hours and more by using two or more ridesharing platforms (Uber, Lyft, and Juno). There is no onus on ridesharing companies to do anything about these practices and there is not law that prevents drivers from doing so. Nevertheless, such practices were found to be necessary in a sector that does not offer conventional full-time employment contracts. As Berger et al. (2018) note, precarious conditions such as these can create anxiety for drivers who find value in the flexibility of ridesharing work but who also need to make a reasonable and sustainable income (see also Chan, 2019).

In our ethnographic study of Uber drivers in London we found drivers to be working a mixture of part- and full-time hours as they tried to fit driving in and around other work, study, and family commitments.[8] Some weeks drivers would work 50+ hours a week and at other times only 20. Though none of the drivers we spoke to were involved in any of the labour disputes in London, they did recognise the ways that Uber incentivises their working practices and nudges them into action, which did encourage them to spend more time using the app over the course of a shift. Genci, an Albanian immigrant driving approximately 40 hours a week, spoke of the trip targets and automatic trip finder that keeps drivers working:

> We get alerts when we log in or out that tell us we'll get a bonus if get enough trips done. It can be fun to try and get these bonuses and it is easy on some days, like a Friday night if you're willing to work late, but sometimes it's not going to happen – they're too hard to reach even if you drive like a madman…There's also this thing that happens when you finish a trip; the app tries to find you another one, like whether you like it or not. I've been kind of trapped by this before and it gets to the point where you have to say no more, you know.
>
> (Genci, March 2015)

Uber has been public about these practices, being quoted as saying:

> We show drivers areas of high demand or incentivize them to drive more. But any driver can stop work literally at the tap of a button — the decision whether or not to drive is 100 percent theirs.
> (Scheiber, 2nd April 2017)

As shown in studies of gamification and interface design, addictive elements are often intentionally designed into digital systems (Schüll, 2012). Ridesharing apps in particular are being designed to manipulate and hold driver attention for as long as possible (Calo and Rosenblat, 2017). This quote from Uber openly acknowledges this, but it does not address how these addictive design practices make tapping the off button increasingly difficult. Without denying the agency of drivers, there are clearly psychological impacts to the way ridesharing apps are designed to lead drivers towards certain ways of working.

Pay has also been central to the regulatory battles around ridesharing platforms. Drivers are lured in with sign-up bonuses and achievable targets, only for these to dry up and become unachievable after a few months.[9] This can leave drivers on wages significantly below their initial expectations, particularly for those that do not have the option to chase the rider targets set by the platforms. Calls for a minimum wage for drivers are becoming common as drivers see real declines in their take-home pay after expenses, increases in Uber's commission and a rise in the number of drivers entering the market.[10] This has led to wide-spread protests and boycotts of ridesharing by drivers, and we are beginning to see unionising as a strategy for drivers looking for collective action around fair pay.[11] In New York, these calls were answered in January 2019 when the city introduced a minimum wage of $17.22 for ridesharing drivers. This is, however, an exception to the rule and for many full-time drivers it remains a struggle to earn a reasonable *and* consistent living through ridesharing. In the London, our drivers said they could earn between £10–15 an hour after expenses when there was a good supply of riders, but it was not uncommon for them to earn as little as £6–7 an hour after expenses during quiet periods. When we compare this with the UK's minimum wage of £7.83 (2018/2019) and the London 'living wage'[12] of £10.25 (2018/2019), we can see that for these drivers their wages fluctuate between below the national minimum wage and above the London living wage. As Martin, a British driver from London stated, this had an impact on how he budgeted for the week and how he made future plans.

> Some weeks are great and I make loads [of money]. I can do everything I want and more then – buy good food, have a blow out, put some in my savings. But when things are slow it can be a struggle just to make it through the week, and when this happens, when I've got bills and stuff to pay it's, well, really stressful isn't it?
> (Martin, June 2015)

One of the ways these drivers tried to keep their pay consistent was to ensure that their driver rating (out of 5 stars) was as high as possible. The logic was that higher ratings would amount to more trust amongst riders, which would translate into more fares for drivers. All of these drivers were aware that without consistently high ratings of 4.6 stars and above, they were liable to be barred from the platform. As with many of Uber's practices, how the ratings system works is a mystery to drivers (and riders) because the company does not release information on how ratings are calculated. Though rating employees in the workplace is nothing new, this has led some to examine how the opacity of Uber's ratings system gets bound up in a politics of gender and race (Rosenblat et al., 2016), labour surveillance (Chan, 2019; Gandini, 2018) and how it has produced a culture of gaming the system, where drivers try all sorts of tactics to generate and maintain a positive rating (Rosenblat, 2018; Scheiber, 2017). Chen (2018) suggests that digital platforms are always spaces of contentious labour politics, with ridesharing drivers making significant efforts to resist and game the technology that creates their conditions of employment. The Uber drivers we spoke with were certainly keen to point out that they were not without agency, which was made clear by the tactics they used to mitigate the effects of the ratings systems. Similar sentiments are also regularly made on uberpeople.net, therideshareguy.com and The Ride Share Guy podcast, which have become popular spaces for drivers wanting to discuss and get tips on how to game the app.

In order to keep his driver rating above 4.8 stars, a threshold he deemed achievable and sustainable, Adedayo, a Nigerian medical student studying in London, employed a number of neutralising tactics to try and encourage high ratings from riders. He always tried to be kind and welcoming, but not annoying, and he would engage in conversation if that's what the passenger wanted, but he would not initiate it. Moreover, he enjoyed having a joke with passengers but was wary to keep his political views to himself so as to not offend passengers, which he thought might lead to a bad rating. Overall, we could say that Adedayo's approach aligned with the old adage that "the customer always knows best", a finding which Chan (2019) suggests is a coercive and self-disciplining workplace performance common amongst Uber drivers. Conversely, Martin had different tactics. He only picked up riders with high ratings and kept things as professional as possible.

> First off, I just keep it professional, you know. No chit-chat, no messing around with routes, no driving like an idiot, but saying yes to reasonable requests. That usually works for me. Then I set a minimum passenger rating. I won't pick up anyone below 4.5 [stars]. There's no point. They'll be annoying and probably give you a crap rating – it's not worth it to get a "paxhole" [term used to describe a bad passenger]. There are always problems – they make stupid demands and are unreasonable about everything. Sometimes it can mean less takings on one night but if it means I keep a high rating I usually make it up the next night.
>
> (Martin, May 2015)

Despite these practices, the drivers did acknowledge that their power to challenge the strategies of Uber was limited and that their work was subject to forces beyond their control and understanding. Most felt cheated by the system, but had nonetheless accepted it and were happy enough to continue the "rating game" (Chan, 2019), at least while money was coming in. As Anthony, a long-term Uber driver from London, put it:

> I personally think Uber messes with the ratings depending on how long you've worked for them. I've been doing this for around 3 years and can't get past 4.84 no matter what I do. They [Uber] say that it's only based on the last 500 rides but that's got to be bullshit. I don't see me ever getting 5 stars anymore.
> (Anthony, February 2015)

As long as the ratings system continues to evolve as a black-box for drivers, they will never know precisely how Uber calculates their rating, which will likely mean that drivers continue trying to game the system. As we have shown, these "monitored performances" (Anderson, 2016) create both precarious conditions of employment as drivers try what they can to keep ratings high, and feelings of anxiety as drivers worry about being barred from the platform as a result of low ratings. Central to these issues is the mass of data, which is collected from drivers and riders, and operationalised by algorithmic systems to determine ratings, as well as driver-rider matches, routes, and pricing. If we are to consider regulating this sector then we must also think through the ways that data is put to use by algorithmic systems (Pasquale, 2015).

Automated "surge pricing", or what's sometimes called "dynamic pricing" offers another good example of how opaque algorithmic systems operationalise data in the ridesharing sector. Surge pricing is when the cost of ridesharing for passengers rises for a period of time when the demand for riders exceeds available drivers in a geographically defined area. This often happens during busy times of the day, such as during the morning and evening commute and once large social events are finished. The cost of trips, the duration of the surge period, the geographical boundaries and how drivers are alerted to surge pricing are automated by algorithmic systems and machine learning artificial intelligence (A.I.) that process driver and passenger data in real-time. As described by our participants, the impact is manifold. It raises prices for passengers using a multiplier model ($x2$, $x3$, $x4$... the standard rate), which makes it financially attractive to drivers and creates a temporary top-end market of riders that can afford the increased fares. It draws drivers from elsewhere in the city and encourages them to anticipate where surge pricing will occur, and it has a direct impact on local taxi markets also looking for business in the area. Moreover, because the automated processes behind surge pricing are neither transparent or accessible to drivers and riders, these impacts are beholden to unknown spatial and temporal rhythms, which can add further anxiety for drivers seeking out riders, and for riders who need to use the service but find it prohibitively expense for a time.

Algorithmic systems are being employed to manipulate drivers and riders with the primary purpose of extracting real-time surplus value in the form of revenues and data. This is shared mobility at its most profit hungry and least socially just. If we consider the goals of mobility justice, there is a strong argument that these forms of ridesharing management should be looked at more closely by regulators because algorithmic and machine learning A.I. systems are not neutral. In the case of surge pricing these systems are primarily being used to produce temporary markets for maximum value extraction. The precarious cultures of practice and social inequalities that follow the implementation of such systems are not yet adequately considered by ridesharing companies or regulators. To date, regulators have yet to fully engage with the relational impacts of surge pricing on drivers working practices, rider experience and city districts. Instead, any regulations put in place have been economically driven to avoid what's known as "price gouging", which are pricing strategies that disproportionally cause market disruption. This was the case in New York, where Uber and regulators agreed on a maximum surge level of $2.5x$ the normal rate after Mayor Bill de Blasio threatened sanctions against the company for creating artificial markets.

Thus far we have shown that shared mobility and especially ridesharing services have become new sites for discussion and contestation around labour. The debates over what constitutes labour, full-time employment and labour management in the digital age will likely continue as we try to understand the impact of on-demand platforms services and the gig work that has become central to the sharing economy.

Data regulation

Collected, stored, analysed, and acted upon data has clearly become central to our interactions with shared mobility whether we are using these services as passengers, drivers, or riders. User data, location

Regulation, platform governance, and labour practices 67

data, financial data, and meta data are just some of the ways we might categorise the data (Kitchin, 2014) that is being collected by these platforms. There is a growing debate on the ethical codes and practices of data collection, storage, and use within the sharing economy sector (Pankratz et al., 2018), which are mirrored in wider discourses around data privacy and data ethics. Discussion of data are attracting a lot of attention from national and international policymakers seeking to challenge how and why user data is being operationalised in contemporary life (Leenes et al., 2018).

The regulation of data in the sector is important because of the power data has in shaping the future of mobility practices. Shared mobility accumulates vast amounts of data about user demographics, preferences, urban travel patterns, and spatio-temporal rhythms, which are immensely valuable for these companies and increasingly for transport and urban planners. This has created tensions between services who claim ownership of it and regulatory authorities who see permission to access this data as essential in planning for the future of cities. Until recently, this data was not been widely shared with planners based on the grounds that shared mobility platforms have proprietary ownership of this data. Moreover, the transnational operations of platforms ensure that the command and control practices of traditional state regulation are not easily enforceable for data practices because data may be extracted from one jurisdiction and analysed in another (Miller, 2015).

Nevertheless, we have recently seen a shift in this model on two fronts. First, regulators have begun demanding access to company data as a condition for operating in their jurisdiction. This has happened in Egypt, where regulators have demanded access to data from Uber and Careem as a condition of granting ridesharing licenses, and in London where Transport for London have made data sharing a key part of their policy statement on private hire services (TFL, 2018).[13] Second, shared mobility services are instigating data sharing practices as a means to create "public-private partnerships" with city authorities (Susha et al., 2017). Both Lime in Lisbon, and Uber in Bogotá, Boston, London, and Nice now share (some of) their data with these city's planners in a bid to build trusting relationships.[14] This is a significant for it signals a shift away from the disruptive model of acting now and apologising later, towards a collaborative model, whereby services and regulators can work together to address transport and planning issues. However, it could be suggested that this is just another leveraging tactic to keep these services in the city at the expense of only minor changes to how they operate. For example, in Boston, under the

Uber Movement initiative, Uber agreed to begin sharing anonymised ZIP Code Tabulation Areas (ZCTA) data, including time-stamped data about when and where trips began and ended, their duration and the distance travelled with the Massachusetts Bay Transportation Authority (MBTA) in 2015. The aim being that the MBTA could understand the travel patterns of its residents and visitors, and plan future transportation and infrastructure accordingly. Whilst this data partnership was initially praised as a new way for ridesharing and cities to work together (Dunca, 2015), it soon became clear that the data sets, organised by ZIP Code rather than individual streets, were too broad to gleam any meaningful insights from (Vaccaro, 2016). When we know Uber's "God View" (a programme that live-tracks all drivers and riders) exits (Bhuiyan and Warzel, 2014), it's hardly surprising that the city of Boston felt short-changed by the limited data sets they had access to.

As long as mobility data remains socially and economically valuable, it will continue to play a role in the future of shared mobility and how it is regulated. We live in a world where the datafication of goods, services and people is increasingly utilised by companies and cities trying to gleam a better understanding of their customers and citizens, now and for the future (Kitchin, 2014; Leszczynski, 2016). Nevertheless, aside from a few case studies, it is not yet clear how this data will be leveraged by platforms and regulators for mobility planning. As Van Dijck et al. (2018) have suggested, there are important questions to be asked about the ongoing datafication of the transport sector, particularly about how this transformation is shaping the social and civic value of public transport as a common good. If shared mobility continues to proliferate in the private sector, we must begin to ask to what extent these services are eroding the long-held goals of public services. What is important is that we start to have a conversation about how data is currently being collected and used in this context, and how it might be used to foster new forms of socially and sustainably responsible mobility services. The datafication of transport is not the problem per se, rather it is the ways in which this data is operationalised that is a cause for concern. Part of the fight for our right to shared mobility is a fight for how our data is being used to shape the future of urban mobility. Regulation in the form of the recent EU General Data Protection Regulation (GDPR) is perhaps the most significant step taken by an international regulatory body so far in response to these issues.[15] Much of its significance has been to start a public conversation about data, which we hope will continue in the coming years.

Data alone will not solve mobility injustice, for this will need broader social and political will, but data can play an important role in highlighting where action needs to be taken. Public MaaS initiatives (see the MaaS Alliance) and commoning open-data (Bingham-Hall, 2016) projects across the world offer a useful testbed for this. The networked and real-time data collected from these services could be used to understand the demands for mobility provision and access, for example who and where needs mobility services and what types of services are needed. CityMapper and SWVL have already begun rolling out mobility services based on this premise, albeit within the private sector. The CityMapper Ride service in London,[16] for example, uses mobility data that indicates where there is a demand but no supply for a bus service to determine where to set up a bus service. This service, operating much like a ridesharing service but along a set route, demonstrates how data can lead to more efficient mobility options. However, it would be difficult to argue that this private service is responding to the issues of mobility justice for it is a service that currently only operates in the city centre, only runs in the evenings and weekends, requires some knowledge of how the system works, costs more than public services and puts additional vehicles on the road.

Realising the potential of sharing mobility as a socially responsible and sustainable mode of transport will require regulators to engage much more closely with the work that algorithmically automated systems do operationalising the data from services. Regulators will therefore need to take a greater interest in the technological processes that underpin these services, and also in the sociological impacts of these systems. As we have seen elsewhere, such as in the aftermath of the Cambridge Analytica and Facebook scandal, when regulators have come up against digital platforms they are often proven to be ill-equipped in understanding how the technology works and what its far reaching sociological impacts are. As we shall demonstrate in the following section, this has come to benefit platforms, who often insist that they are in the best position to mitigate the social impacts of their technology because they built it.

New directions for regulation

One of the ways that shared mobility platforms insist they can offer safe and sustainable transport solutions without affecting innovation and economic growth is through self-regulation. The notion of letting the market regulate itself is very popular across the technology sector, and there are numerous cases where platforms have attempted to sell the idea of self-regulation to consumers and regulators through marketing and lobbying campaigns (Witt et al., 2015). This is usually done through public assertations that platforms are in the best position to regulate themselves, through the creation of public-private partnerships or through industry-organised regulatory bodies that create principles and guidelines (but not always laws) that platforms sign up to. A clear example of the former is the way that Uber has responded to cases of driver and ride assaults, whereby it has continued to offer reassurances to legislators that it is making significant steps in self-regulating its platform through tougher driver screening processes. An example of the latter is the creation of the TNCs network in California set up in 2013 by the California Public Utilities Commission (CPUC). This organisation was set up to create standards that services should adhere to, but which are enforced by the platforms themselves rather than the state. These self-regulatory practices have proved to be some what successful model for platforms, with the majority seemingly able to convince regulators that self-regulation is working.

Shared mobility platforms have used this model when responding to the concerns of vehicle emissions and driver/passenger safety raised by city authorities around the world. For example, in response to regulatory threats or in anticipation of regulatory measures, ridesharing platforms Lyft (USA) and Uber (worldwide, but not in every country of operation) now have policies which stipulate that drivers must drive low or zero emission vehicles by 2020. There have also been considerable efforts from these companies to improve the security checks that new drivers must pass before than can begin work.[17] Barring some notable exceptions, shared mobility platforms have been able to produce relatively safe spaces of transit through these checks and the rating systems they use, whereby platforms ask drivers and riders to rate one another in an exercise of peer-to-peer regulation. These practices are used as exemplars to demonstrate how ridesharing firms are actively responding to the concerns raised. By doing so they add further evidence that supports the notion of that self-regulation is an effective alternative to legal regulation.

Nevertheless, when we take a step back to examine where the costs and associated labour of these practices are being drawn from, we can see that it is the drivers of these services and not the platforms themselves where the burdens of self-regulation are placed. Indeed, it is the drivers that must purchase (or rent) and maintain their low or zero emissions vehicle, and as we discussed above, it is drivers that are responsible for the labour associated with maintaining a high rating in a system with unclear guidance on what constitutes a good rating

Regulation, platform governance, and labour practices 71

and how to achieve it. In effect, ridesharing platforms are promoting the message that they are engaging in effective self-regulation, but in reality the responsibility of these measures are primarily passed on to drivers, with riders also contributing labour in their role as ratings agents.

The self-regulatory practices of platforms have been noticeably weak when it comes to addressing the issues over labour, congestion, accessibility, user data, and service provision for marginal groups, all of which are key if we are to realise the potential of sharing mobility as a socially responsible and sustainable mode of transport. Self-regulation is supported by the economic promise of the sharing economy, which as we have argued alongside others, has been co-opted and misused by platforms who have very little interest in promoting true cultures of sharing (Katrini, 2018). As we have seen in reference to Uber over the past few years, self-regulation has been self-serving rather than socially serving. Time and again, digital platforms make apologies and apply retrospective technological solutions for their actions. This suits platforms because they evade regulatory measures that might challenge their market practices (Witt et al., 2015).

In response to the pitfalls of state and self-regulation there has been a growing interest in developing alternative models of regulation in the sector. These include the models of transparent and shared-regulation (Balaram, 2016; Cohen and Sundararajan, 2017), anticipatory regulation (Armstrong et al., 2019), and data-led regulation (Johal and Zon, 2015; Steenhoven et al., 2016). Each of these models, though different, can be characterised by their promise to include a range of stakeholders and develop iterative measures, employ recursive approaches to regulation and to use data in decision making. Involving a diverse group of stakeholders in the regulatory process is said to allow more voices to be heard, different concerns to be raised and for an altogether more democratic approach to regulation. Balaram (2016) suggests this could mean working with policymakers, legal and administrative professionals, investors, business leaders, designers, community organisers, users, and platforms. The aim is to design common goals based on stakeholder interests and ultimately to distribute the responsibility and power for regulating the sector beyond policymakers and platforms.

Iterative and recursive regulatory models are based on the idea that regulation needs to be dynamic by design in order to keep pace with the frequent changes in technologies and market practices. This can mean the periodic reviewing of legislation and making decisions based on the analysis of data provided by platforms or from independent sources (Armstrong et al., 2019). However, iterative models are challenging and not yet widely used because regulation can take a long time to pass through legislative channels and is not easily undone or changed once it's implemented.

Data-led decision-making offers an interesting way forward for regulation. As we saw above, public-private data partnerships between platforms and regulators could be used to better understand and manage the impact that these services have. However, there are also dangers here too, with private companies not wanting to relieve control of valuable and powerful data sets and because a reliance on data-led solutions tends to lead to technocratic solutions to social issues. Following critiques of the so-called "smart city" (Kitchin et al., 2017), it would be a mistake to assume data-led decision making can be used to regulate the socio-technical landscape of shared mobility.

In the context of shared mobility these regulatory models could amount for a significant shift in current practices, where it is clear that regulatory efforts are self-serving (for platforms and the regulators), inefficient, do not respond to the diversity of sharing services and can move quickly out of date. In particular, the desire to design social inclusion into these models of regulation rather than as something to be applied retrospectively is a positive step forward, if it can be realised in practice. However, we argue that a different approach is needed, which takes these regulatory models into account, but is focused on realising the potential sharing mobility for developing mobility justice. This, we argue, will take us away from regulatory models that address transportation and economic concerns to one that also takes into consideration the social and environmental impacts of sharing mobility.

Towards relational regulation

> ...the urban mobility revolution has been dominated by transport network companies (TNCs) that utilize mobile apps or websites to pair drivers with passengers. They have largely emerged without holistic thinking about how they integrate with other public services and meet the mobility needs of cities as a whole.
>
> (Ede, 2018: 62)

Here, Ede gets to the heart of why some form of regulation is necessary if we are to realise the potential of these services for tackling the issues of mobility justice. It urges us to think more about the networks of relations that constitute contemporary shared mobility; to consider the bigger picture of how these services are impacting not only on urban transportation, but also far wider social, political, economic, and environmental practices. This follows the notion that (im)mobility is always a relational issue, as we discussed in Chapter 3 (see also Nikolaeva et al., 2019; Sheller, 2018).

The principle of *relational regulation*, asks that we adopt a networked approach to regulating the sector.[18] We suggest that mapping out the affected actors of shared mobility and then examining the strength of relations between them will help regulators and platforms understand the broader impacts of their actions. As we have demonstrated throughout this book, sharing mobility does not happen in isolation. It is not simply a new form of transportation. Instead it is an emerging form of mobility that is part of and affects a network of actors (people, cultures, attitudes, regulation, products, ideas, technologies, pollutants, platforms, cities, working practices, etc.), all of which can be locally and globally interconnected in different ways. Current regulations of shared mobility are, by contrast, generally geared towards addressing single issues such as emissions, safety, labour rights, or service competition. This certainly can be effective in the short term (the New York Uber case is evidence of this), but more could be done to address how these issues relate to one another and to the wider social and material networks of which they are a part of over the long term. This is particularly important if we see the future of sharing mobility as a way to address the issues of mobility (in)justice, where the problems are not easily solved by regulating for single issues.

There are relational models of shared mobility regulation already in operation, but they are focused on transportation issues. Take the case of Sao Paulo, where the city regulates TNCs (including ridesharing services) through a "a pay as you drive" mechanism where drivers must pay mileage fees to the city for the cost and maintenance of road infrastructure. This form of regulation has been praised by transport planners and policymakers as a way to mitigate the relational impacts that TNCs have on congestion and driving infrastructures (see for example Darido, 2016). However, we argue it doesn't go far enough in tackling the wider connections between labour, road infrastructure, and the environment. It is the drivers, who already suffer under their employment conditions, who pay for this charge and not the platform operators. Moreover, the recuperated costs from this regulation are primarily used to pay for road repairs rather than support sustainable transport infrastructure. An approach with mobility justice in mind would seek to impose regulations that ensure drivers are paid a fair wage, that platforms pay a significant contribution to these costs, and that these fees are directly invested into sustainable transport schemes.

More effective relational regulation of ridesharing platforms could be used, for example, to tackle how vehicle emissions and traffic congestion relate to labour rights. Emissions could be kept lower by giving drivers the status of employees, a salary, and a holding taxi rank. This could mitigate the current practice of driving around until notified of a job or joining a procession of cars on their way to a surge-pricing hotspot, which drives up emissions, congestion, and driver anxiety. Regulating the ridesharing sector without taking these relations into account can have a detrimental effect on drivers. If regulation means individual drivers are penalised, rather than the operating company, like they currently are in London's £12.50 emissions charge for Private Hire Vehicles (PHV), then regulation is not working towards mobility justice. Introducing this emissions tax will likely reduce emissions from PHV, but it is drivers, due to their employment status as self-employed contractors (or "partners") rather than employees who will pay the price for these taxes. By following a relational approach to regulation there are alternative ways to bring down emissions whilst not penalising drivers, but they will require that we legitimately recognise the work and financial commitments of drivers, and how this effectively subsidises end-user costs.

The principles of relational regulation can also be applied to regulating data and algorithmic practices in the sector. These digital processes can lead to real-time price hikes, transit deserts, and precarious working conditions, all of which can (re)produce mobility injustices around who gains to benefit from using these services and who does not. Regulation that takes into account the relational effects of these digital processes will be essential in tackling the social impacts that are often concealed by the interfaces of shared mobility platforms. This will require independent regulatory bodies that understand how these systems operate to work closely to social scientists studying the impacts of these systems. It will also mean working with digital platforms to develop an auditing culture that is not yet prevalent within the technology sector.

The limitations of a relational approach are clear in the current climate. It would require a radical shift in regulatory practices and politics, where the onus is on facilitating economic growth above all else. It would also require a cultural shift, both in our understanding of the hidden impacts of on-demand mobility services, and our desire to act responsibly on this knowledge. This does not mean that relational approaches to regulation are not possible, but it does mean compromises and sacrifices will be necessary. The question is then how to make a successful economic and cultural case for relational regulation in the sector. Without making these regulatory measures attractive to the disruptive business model and our appetite for on-demand services, it's difficult to see the sector adopting this approach if it means affecting the current rates of growth and the practices of participation.

One of the ways forward could lie in educating platforms, policymakers and users of shared mobility about how the sector impacts on wider networks of relations. This could lead to calls for, and enforcement of, more stringent practices of social responsibility by companies within the sector. To avoid practices similar to that of "green-washing", companies could be legally bound to sign up for certification schemes that encourage more socially and sustainably just mobilities. The Fairwork Foundation, for example, has recently been established to develop an independent certification model focused on labour practices in the gig economy, including ridesharing drivers.[19] They apply a certification score to platforms based on if they meet a set of interrelated requirements including fair pay, fair working conditions, fair contracts, fair management, and fair representation. By doing so they are effectively applying a relational approach to certification that supports the goals of mobility justice. It is too early to tell if this scheme will be effective (launched in March 2019), but it does have great potential for the shared mobility sector. Consumers could also make use of their purchasing power, recognising that withholding their participation from services can lead to change. Well publicised consumer boycotts and lobbying could be a useful tactic for raising awareness about the relational effects of sharing mobility. In the case of Uber's treatment of workers, this has worked to some extent, with the #DeleteUber campaign leading to some positive changes within sector around driver and passenger safety.

Ultimately, for the principles of relational regulation to be taken seriously, there will need to be a period of experimentation in real-world cases to establish what works and what does not in terms of a networked approach to regulation. As we have demonstrated in this chapter, regulation of the sector is anything but simple. Nevertheless, we believe that this approach offers a good starting point for thinking about how to regulate for the broader interconnected impacts of sharing mobility.

Notes

1 Except wheelchair accessible ridesharing vehicles.
2 Uber only began to turn a profit in 2018, and there is still much speculation as to whether the company can sustain profitability at its current rate of expansion.

3 This model is often associated with Joseph Schumpeter's economic model of 'creative destruction', which seeks to create and maintain capital growth through the continual disruption of existing markets (McCraw, 2010).
4 Ex-policy-lobbying appears to becoming a trend in the technology industry. For example, former UK prime minister David Cameron now chairs the advisory board of Afiniti, an AI company, and former UK deputy prime minister Nick Clegg now works for Facebook as its head of global affairs and communication.
5 www.austinchronicle.com/daily/news/2017-03-14/lege-for-sale/.
6 The labour disputes around ridesharing pertain to a number of important issues, including but not limited to: gendered and racial divides, the health and corporeal practices of drivers, and the safety of drivers and riders.
7 Reliable statistics are difficult to obtain from Uber, who have been reluctant to reveal driver numbers and hours worked unless pushed by regulators. These figures were only revealed after a parliamentary select committee (2017) ordered uber to provide clarification. https://parliamentlive.tv/Event/Index/e1e66f5d-7a50-46d0-a0a6-b998f696d32c.
8 For the period of seven months between February and September 2015, I met monthly (approximately) with four participating Uber drivers in London. They were initially recruited during conversations as a passenger in their cars. The quotes and observations included here were taken from interviews and 'ride-alongs' with the drivers as well from conversations we had via email and social media. All driver names have been anonymised using pseudonyms to protect the privacy of these participants. For comparative studies, see Eisenmeier's (2018) case study of Uber in Mexico City and Rosenblat's (2018) impressive study of Uber drivers in the US and Canada.
9 Uber's driver rewards program is one example of this. Uber Pro, as it's called, is a set of incentives designed to encourage drivers onto the platform. These include 'quest promotions' (trip targets), discounts on vehicle maintenance and road-side recovery, and educational support for drivers wanting to earn qualifications whilst they drive. See www.uber.com/us/en/drive/uber-pro/.
10 To offer and example, Uber reports that the number of US drivers has gone from 160,000 in 2014 to 900,000 in 2018 (Mishkin, 2018).
11 See, for example, the work of the Independent Workers Union of Great Britain.
12 The recommended but not enforced minimum wage for London workers. See www.livingwage.org.uk/calculation.
13 In the Egypt case, requirements for data have gone as far as demanding ridesharing services host their data servers within Egypt and share data with security services (Walsh, 2017).
14 www.uber.com/en-IE/newsroom/publictransit/.
15 See https://eugdpr.org.
16 Formally CityMapper Smartbus.
17 That said, the stringency of these security checks continues to be called into question as high profile cases of sexual abuse and violence by drivers

continue to be reported regularly in the press. High profile cases include the rape of an unnamed woman by her Uber driver, Shiv Kumar Yadav, in Delhi in 2014, and the rape of a 26-year-old unnamed women by her Uber driver, Frederick Gaston, in Miami in 2017.
18 This approach draws from relational frameworks such as actor-network theory (see Latour, 2005), which emphasise the relations between actors in a network.
19 https://fair.work.

5 Empowering connections
Relations, collaborations, and community in sharing mobility

Struggling between ME and WE in the sharing economy

The dualistic tension between ME and WE is at the core of the sharing economy. The title of the pioneering book, "What's mine is yours" by Botsman and Rogers (2010), the reverse provocation of "What's yours is mine" by Slee (2017), and Benkler's (2004) definition of the sharing economy as "pro-social" behaviour all emphasise this dualism. When we begin to explore the tension of this dualism, we can see that the sharing economy is at once pulling users towards individualised practices of consumption, labour, and exchange, and at the same time towards collective practices and imaginations of networked communities.

The sharing economy, at least theoretically, or in the public narrative, is opposed to the normal systems of linear production and the distribution of goods and services through the promotion of an alternative model that reintroduces the value of concepts such as reuse, equity, and, above all, community. In this sense it takes inspiration from the gift economy (Mauss, 1924; Polanyi 1957; Simmel, 1950) and networked communities that distribute social capital and trust (Coleman 1988; Fukuyama, 1995; Granovetter 1985). Consistent with the Maussian or Simmellian analysis of gift exchange, the "sharing" that characterises the sharing economy cannot always be defined as a spontaneous gesture of solidarity, for it is also a coercive practice and a reciprocal scheme that is not exclusively unconditional. As Benkler (2004) notes, the exchange model of sharing does not prevent possible transaction costs or selective exclusionary processes, as in the more traditional models of market exchange.

Despite the promises of re-embedding social life into the economy, it is difficult to conclude that a true collaborative movement has come to fruition (Schor, 2014), even if there are some planted seeds, like the

Shareable group,[1] the P2P Foundation,[2] the Co-City group in Turin[3] and Bologna, or the Platform Cooperative movement.[4] Instead, what has come to the fore is a sharing economy based on a platform model of market disruption backed by venture capital. This is now the perception of the sharing economy's potential in the world. As the data presented in Chapter 2 showed, sharing mobility is now a key part of platform capitalism.

Nevertheless, sociability and sharing have still become intrinsic to the organisational paradigm of the digital platform. This is because platforms enable the interaction between two or more groups of actors (Srnicek, 2016). Due the size and growth of this sector, evaluating the opportunities to socialise and share under this paradigm continue to be an area for sociological research and analysis. Many of the contributions thus far have focused on the issue of the motivation(s) to share rather than on the concrete practices of social interaction and sharing. As Belk (2014) has pointed out, there is still a need to understand how the sharing economy could offer spaces to help and develop human connections inasmuch as it can facilitate access to new spaces of economic exchange.

Recent analysis has highlighted how low-quality social capital can be produced under the conditions of the sharing economy (Bardhi and Eckhardt, 2012; Fenton, 2013; Parigi and State, 2014). The interactions are said to be predominantly instrumental and pragmatic, and do not tend to develop into a deeper sociality (Arcidiacono and Podda, 2017). This limited sociability is attractive to sharing platforms because when exchange relationships do recur, users tend to bypass or substitute the brokering work done by the platform. When studies have examined the types of sociability practiced on sharing platforms, they have found that homophily in class, race and cultural capital are prominent factors in determining who is involved in these interactions. This has been the case for digital time banking systems, where users tend to prefer trading with others of the same social status and with the same cultural capital (Dubois et al., 2014; Pais and Del Maral, 2018). It has also been the case for Airbnb users, where race and class have been factors in determining how people interact when using the service (Edelman et al., 2017). With this in mind, can we say the same for digitised mobility practices? What can we say about sociability within the context of sharing mobility?

Relations on the move: ME and WE in sharing mobility

Historically, the relation between sociality and transport has been underestimated in the academic and public debate, which has usually given more attention to systemic issues (i.e. urban planning, urban quality of life, service accessibility, environmental impact, etc.). However, recent studies criticise the notion that mobility is a neutral phenomenon, concerned only with factors such as time, cost, and access (Jensen et al., 2014; Rubin, 2015; Urry, 2000). These studies urge us instead, to treat mobility as a relational phenomenon, where the time, cost, and access of mobility are socially produced and mediated through human relationships, because we are all "linked-in-motion" (Brömmelstroet et al., 2017: 4).

In the experiences of sharing mobility, we do find elements of sociality, although these are markedly different depending on the type of service in question. Interactions and relationships generated from sharing mobility can be the source of a social bond, as mainly expressed in carpooling experiences, but they can also remain simply an experiential factor that enriches the practice of consumption, such as can be seen in ridesharing services. In order to clarify the impact of sharing mobility on social relations, it can be useful to refer to the typology elaborated by Pais and Provasi (2015), which complete the Polanyian taxonomy alongside market, redistribution, and reciprocity. According to the two Italian scholars, using the Polanian taxonomy can be useful for understanding the peculiarities of services in the sharing economy. There is a need, they suggest, to reclassify these economic exchange practices by introducing two new exchange systems: *collaboration* and *common pooling*.

Collaboration is based on a general form of knowledge about social transactions, which is different to knowledge about market transactions. Collaborations unfold within grey areas, where formal and informal rules determine, limit, and discipline social interactions. These are different to market transactions where constraints are more strictly controlled by law. Furthermore, in a collaboration, assets must be sharable and not seen as the exclusive property of the service provider, nor can the transaction be exclusively based on money. Symbolic capital, such as digital reputation mechanisms, is equally valued as a medium of exchange. However, there are also many things in common between collaboration and market transactions. For example, the reasons for interactions are mainly extrinsic; the exchange relationship is symmetrical; commitment rates among actors are low.

Common pooling is profoundly different from collaboration. Transactions are based on a reciprocal knowledge that derives from belonging to some form of community. The lever of identity is fundamental as a mechanism of adhesion and motivation, and also as a constraint within the exchange process. Regulated by communitarian rules, common pooling is defined by a high level of commitment based on loyalty and retention rates amongst participants. The principles of resource allocation are based on mutuality and the means of transactions are mediated by personal status within the community. In the following, we apply these two concepts to the different forms of sharing mobility to highlight the significant differences in sociality across the sharing mobility landscape.

In general, users of sharing mobility based on peer-to-peer models enter into a relationship with each other, get to know each other, and enjoy the pleasure of making a reciprocal exchange that takes place without the intervention of any vertical mediator (Bardhi and Eckhardt, 2012). In this sense, it can be said that many forms of sharing mobility intrinsically possess the social value found in collaborative and common pooling, even when the exchange is mediated by money. However, when we consider services outside of the peer-to-peer configuration, such as vehicle sharing services, it is the market trade system, rather than collaboration or common pooling that is more popular.

Car/bike sharing is a predominantly market-based service with an individual fruition model based on an impersonal relationship between a user and a provider. For example, a study of car sharing in Milan showed that 66% of respondents to a web survey on a representative sample of Car2go users, used the vehicle alone and did not share it with anyone else, despite price incentives for pooling (Arcidiacono and Pais, 2018). This highlights a low level of collaboration or common pooling between users and therefore suggests that, for car sharing, sociality is expressed only in the limited form of a market interaction between a company and a user, where interactions are digitally augmented and kept to a minimum. Moreover, it is not common for users of these services to meet or communicate with each other in their practices of sharing. Instead sharing the asset involves a form of indirect and digitally mediated collaboration, which governs the interaction between the user, the asset, and the company that facilitates these transactions. From these indirect practices of sharing, two main rules can be identified:

- Shared vehicles tend to be left in areas of high demand in the city centre, on pain of paying a surcharge if it is left in a peripheral area, excluded from the core sharing area.
- The vehicles must always be parked in an accessible area to facilitate the exchange process between users.

These two simple rules create many frictions within the Car2go service and become recurring sources of complaint among users (Arcidiacono and Pais, 2017). Compared to the first rule, it is immediately clear that most of the requests coming from customers are concerned with the elimination of the surcharge in the event they left the car in a peripheral area. The recurrence of this complaint calls into question the perceived fairness of this practice, which has an impact on customer satisfaction based on the transparency and costs of the service. Similarly, the second rule is not respected by some users who, in order to ensure that a vehicle is in close proximity for their subsequent needs, leave the car inside private spaces and not in an accessible parking area. It is clear that this is an important violation of the collaborative principle and it testifies the resilience of an individualistic model of consumption.

Moreover, this study also found that many of Car2go customers complained of dirty or neglected vehicles, which they linked to previous users: the assessment of satisfaction recorded with regard to vehicle maintenance and cleaning (in a scale from 1 to 10) reached an average of 6.71 against a total satisfaction level of around 8. In particular, with respect to re-fuelling, users preferred not to collaborate in this process, instead preferring cars with a full tank, even for very short journeys. It is no coincidence that service providers strive to create incentives or sanction systems for these behaviours to minimise their impact on service quality, and yet this research shows that these individualistic practices continue.

In the case of carpooling, the relational aspects of sharing mobility are configured differently. Since the beginning of its development, carpooling has been a system of mobility based on trust relationships, even with its transition from being an informal and casual way for sharing the trip to work among co-workers or family members, to a model based on formal arrangements mediated by software. These trust relations develop over time and are carefully negotiated by users in order to mitigate potential risks. For many passengers using the BlaBlaCar pooling service for the first time, it was found that they preferred to be with a friend or a co-worker, which was said to mitigate the initial fears of travelling alone with a stranger (Setiffi and Lazzer, 2018). It was also found that some drivers made a note on their trip proposal to indicate that they are travelling with their partner, as if to clearly send a message to dissuade unwanted and unrequested attention from prospective passengers (Arcidiacono et al., 2016). However, this initial attitude of distrust and fear towards sharing the trip with a stranger tends to change with the recurrent use of the platform, as Setiffi and Lazzer (2018: 89–90) observe in their study:

Users overcome a state of initial fear and later acquire the skills and knowledge to help them adopt a different approach to the service. Furthermore, they adopt new goals linked to meeting "new friends"... develop new justifications and feelings that still foster mutual collaboration.

This finding is supported by a textual analysis of how users describe and introduce themselves within the BlaBlaCar platform (Arcidiacono et al., 2016). It is evident from this research that the propensity to develop social relations represents the prevailing narrative that unites carpoolers. The most recurrent words from this analysis were; *company* (10.383), *persons* (5944), and *know* (5695). These lemmas are mostly used to describe a sort of inner disposition to sociability and to meet new people among those who offer or seek passage within the platform. Therefore, this disposition to social relations represents the salient element to which most users refer to attract other poolers. This propensity towards sociality occurs abundantly in the user descriptions posted on the platform, for example:

Dear traveller friends, I'm from Cassino but I work in Milan. What to say, I travel a lot, I love being with new and nice people. I have a quiet guide, we stop when you want, always trying to keep the march, but without run so much, so far everyone with a smile got off the car;-).

I wait for you in my car, with the usual bottle of water and candies available for all!

It is also interesting to observe how these social relations were developed during trips and across multiple trips. An interview survey by Arcidiacono et al. (2016) found that 63% of users discussed work and 49% discussed their destination (which remain key reasons for pooling) during trips. Moreover, they found that 47.6% of users discussed the platform and their previous trip experiences. Combined, these common discussions facilitated comfortable social interactions between drivers and passengers. Furthermore, more than half of the users interviewed developed forms of recurrent interaction: 56.4% claimed to have travelled together again and almost a 30% have become friends on Facebook or other social networks. 27.8% even declared the service had facilitated the birth of a new friendship or a recurring social relationship. However, these modes of relationship are not the norm within the platform because more than 80% of overall passengers use the service occasionally and trips are rarely replicated between the two same subjects. Instead, these figures reflect the experiences of heavy users, who show a high level of loyalty to the service. Their loyalty is rewarded by the company through the "ambassador" title, which allows them to be more visible and gain more contacts for pooling. Therefore, the more experienced users develop a peculiar status within the platform whereby building social relations tends to result in a higher user status, which has significant benefits. As Farajallah et al.'s (2016) study of BlaBlaCar suggests, experienced users can negotiate better prices and conditions compared with less experienced consumers. Based on data collected daily between 2013 and 2014, comparing pricing behaviours in France of users on a relatively short trip (Nimes–Montpellier) with users on a relatively long trip (Paris–Marseille), the authors found that drivers with more positive feedback ratings set lower prices and sold more seats. Once they have reached the highest status of ambassador, drivers were perceived to be more experienced, active, and reliable users, which meant they could sell 5% more seats compared to less experienced drivers.

Not only does the status linked to the experience of the carpooler seem to play an important role, but so too does the profile and the homophily of transaction networks. Blumenberg and Smart's (2014) study of carpooling in California found that immigrants were more likely to travel by carpool than US-born citizens. This supports the notion that social bonds between immigrants are developed within communities of practice. In this case, these bonds are developed in carpooling communities where immigrants use their social networks to easily find others in their neighbourhoods to travel with. By contrast, immigrants living in non-immigrant neighbourhoods were found to be less likely to carpool. Cases of the discriminatory effects of homophily have been shown elsewhere, for example, in studies that show users with Arabic-sounding names are less likely to be chosen as drivers in carpooling networks (Farajallah et al., 2016). Collectively, these studies suggest that high levels of homophily exist within carpooling, which is consistent with what has emerged within other sharing services like Airbnb or digital time banks.

What is interesting is how homophily can also be boosted by the platform itself. BlaBlaCar in Italy, for example, launched the "Travel in Pink" initiative in 2015, which is a carpooling service designed to match female drivers with female passengers and their children; the aim being to draw female users onto the platform by mitigating the perceived risk of travelling with people of other gender. Once a ride has been offered, users can choose between the options "normal" (open to all) or "pink", together with other options (smokers or non-smokers, animals allowed or not, etc.). All these possibilities of selection and personalisation of the service do nothing but reinforce the tendency towards homophily as a peculiar feature of sharing services.

In ridesharing systems, this social dimension is not as central as in carpooling and there is little in-depth analysis on this issue. Formal and informal mechanisms of interaction, utilitarianism, and sociality merge in a much more hybridised system that refers closely to the idea of collaboration, as conceptualised by Pais and Provasi (2015). For example, a US study by McKinsey and Company shows that Uber and Lyft passengers are motivated by the convenience of the service (Hensley et al., 2017). The drivers, on the other hand, are motivated above all by economic rather than social factors. Nevertheless, as we discussed in the previous chapter, there is still a strong social component of their labour, which we can see in other jobs where social relations with clients are common (see Hochschild, 1983). Rosenblat et al.'s (2016) study of Uber highlights the psychological frustration that some drivers feel in relation to the rating system, but also their sense of guilt for customer dissatisfaction related to issues such as the music played during the trip, the temperature inside the car, or even the quality of the conversation. In these cases, the homophily of the transaction plays an important role in minimising the risk of client dissatisfaction, but it can also generate problems around accessibility and inclusivity to the service. For example, according to Calo and Rosenblat (2017), riders that are not white have to wait more for a ride when hailing an Uber in Seattle or Boston, which suggests that the preferences of some drivers can produce forms of racial discrimination.

Under these labour conditions, the option to leave the service is often taken up by drivers. This is demonstrated by research on driver satisfaction, which highlights how 68% of Uber's drivers leave the platform after six months (Campbell, 2018). However, other studies suggest that some drivers continue to work because they have some form of dependence on the platform (for example, because it represents the only source of income), which delays their exit (Schor et al., 2018). In reference to the latter, it could be argued that there is a coerced loyalty, particularly for groups such as immigrants who make up much of ridesharing driver labour (PEW, 2016). Many of these drivers use the platform as a way to overcome some of the entry barriers to work in the mobility sector and have become reliant on it for work.

In summary, we can classify the main forms of sharing mobility and their relational impact through three forms of regulation that develop the classification of Pais and Provasi (2015) (see Table 5.1). This comparative table is constructed by taking into *consideration* their

Table 5.1 The types of social relation mapped onto different sharing mobility services

	Vehicle sharing	Carpooling	Ridesharing
Type of economic integration	Market	Common-pooling	Collaboration
Identity	Impersonality	Communitarian belonging	Generic knowledge (through app & reputation devices)
Relationality	Not relevant	Intrinsic feature	Extrinsic feature
Type of relation	B2C	P2P Sharers	Professional-amateur
Spaces of relationality	Indirect occasionally after the trip	Beyond the trip	Exclusively during the trip (as a service feature)
Degree of commitment	Easy exit	Loyalty/affection	Difficult exit
Mediation tool	Money	Status	Reputation
Structure of relations	Low homophily	High homophily	Medium homophily

relational dimensions of reciprocity, market, redistribution, collaboration, and common pooling, and linking them to vehicle sharing, carpooling, and ridesharing.

Vehicle-sharing systems are based mainly on impersonal market relations mediated by money and technology. The traditional exchange structure set up between a provider and a user of a service (business to consumer) is to a large extent now digitally mediated and indirect, which leaves little opportunity for any kind of human mediation. Social interactions only become necessary occasionally, such as when there are complaints to be made, while direct contact with other users is practically absent. Regarding ridesharing services such as Uber or Lyft, we find a hybridised model of relations that is not simply market-led but based on a collaborative structure in which monetary transactions are dynamically mediated and determined by reputational algorithms and a range of social interactions between drivers and passengers. Nevertheless, the pleasant social experiences of ridesharing for both drivers and passengers are but a side effect of this service model. It is unlikely that any meaningful and lasting relations can develop in the short time of a single trip, and even if they are it is unlikely that they will be matched again by the algorithmic systems that pair drivers and passengers. For carpooling, this social dimension is constitutive because this type of service needs the development and consolidation of a trusted social group characterised by the same aims in order to grow. People that supply or use the service have an active role to play in maintaining the effectiveness of this system. Through respectful behaviour, determined by the rules and social norms that discipline the users of these services, significant social relations are incorporated into the quality of the service itself. In some way, the relationship operates upstream and downstream of the service chain: the demand is based on a willingness to interact and relate with other drivers and passengers sharing the travel experience. At the same time, the interactive dynamic has an impact in the construction of future relationships, where more socially active users gain a privileged status within the platform. In the case of carpooling, common rituals, practices, and traditions can generate a sense of belonging and affection towards the service among peers, which are symbolic of an alternative mode of transport. Central to this formation is *trust* and *community*, which we will now discuss in relation to the digital reputation systems favoured by sharing mobility platforms.

A (digital) trust issue

Trust is a form of currency in the platform economy, where it has become essential in enabling transactions among strangers that are not professional providers. The value of this trust-currency is represented by the reputational capital of platforms, which is accumulated as platforms grow their user base by seeking ways to capitalise on the network effects of internet technology (Srnicek, 2016). Simply put, having a higher number of users who exchange increases the reputational capital and the trust in the platform itself, not only for the customer base, but also for investors. However, it is not just the size of the customer base that generates trust in sharing mobility services. Trust is also related to platform design, where users want to trust that the platform will enable successful connections and relations among users. For example, the payment system and how it is designed could make the difference in the process of trust building between users and platforms (Täuscher and Kietzmann, 2017). Carpooling.com, the pioneering German service founded in 2005, initially allowed its users to share their travel expenses in cash. However, in 2013, the platform changed this system by requesting that users pay online in advance and by taking a small percentage of these transactions as a service fee. This change generated a growing dissatisfaction of users, who had already socialised to a different model. This led many to leave the platform and turn to other carpooling sites. Conversely, BlaBlaCar has tried to develop trust by entering into an agreement with AXA insurers to protect drivers from the potential risks of travelling with unknown passengers. By anticipating legislation on the very delicate and controversial issue of consumer protection in sharing services, BlaBlaCar has taken active steps which it hopes will grow a trusting user base.

BlaBlaCar is a valid example of how to build trust among users through effective platform design. Referred to as D.R.E.A.M.S, the company has developed a framework and toolset with the aim of building trust in sharing mobility communities. D.R.E.A.M.S stands for six principles:

- *D-eclared*: those who register in the platform must create a user profile including their name, age, and a short description of themselves.
- *R-ated*: each user is rated by the feedback received from other users. Feedback is expressed in five categories depending on the level of experience: (1) Beginner – users who have recently joined the service, have never used it and do taking a small percentage of the transaction and not have a complete profile with respect to all personal information and preferences requests, (2) Apprentice – users who have a seniority of at least one month, 60% of a full profile and at least 1 positive feedback, (3) Connoisseur – users with a seniority of at least three months and at least three feedbacks, of which more than 70% are positive, (4) Expert – users with a seniority of at least six months and at least six feedbacks, of which more than 80% are positive, (5) Ambassador – users with a seniority of at least one year and at least 12 feedbacks, of which more than 90% are positive. The system asks the user to also declare the level of chat, giving indications to the users of the propensity to socialise and interact during trips. These are based on three ascending levels: bla, blabla, blablabla.
- *E-ngaged*: a booking system based on prepayments made online.
- *A-ctive*: the platform provides information on the user's activity level.
- *M-oderated*: there is a process of verification of the contact information received, such as the telephone number and the bank account used.
- *S-ocial*: the platform allows linking to social networks, such as Facebook and LinkedIn.

The company has verified the impact of this system through research conducted with 18,829 users in 11 European countries (Mazzella and Sundurarajan, 2016). This survey showed that 88% of users trusted

BlaBlaCar, 58% trusted other BlaBlaCar users more than their work colleagues and 42% more than their neighbours. The survey also verified the presence of a brand effect, where BlaBlaCar was +21% more trustworthy compared to another generic mobility service. According to the results of this study, the greater confidence attributed to BlaBlaCar users is said to be largely due to the effectiveness of the platform's reputational system. In this sense, the respect of the rules and its operating logics assume a reassuring function that is reinforced through use, transforming this consumption choice into a true and proper social practice (Setiffi and Lazzer, 2018).

In the sharing economy, and not only in the BlaBlaCar case, trust is also produced through specific digital reputation tools that operate as socio-technical intermediaries between users and platforms (Callon, 1998). The reputation of user-workers on these platforms is formalised through the likes, stars, ratings, and comments, which are used to certify the reliability of the user-worker. Many of these systems are user generated and are used to as a way to reward and discipline each other on the platform. However, these systems are also heavily dependent on an IT architecture, much of which is now algorithmically determined. The result is a reputation system with the appearance of neutrality, but in reality, is a system where the variables that determine user-workers reputation are subject to opaque algorithmic manipulations. Following Pasquale (2015), the reputational system is not neutral, nor even transparent, but rather black-boxed and therefore fundamentally unknowable to the platform user-worker. Indeed, these systems are symbolic of the way that platforms are organised and operate, which is to hide behind the platform's interface.

At the same time as being opaque, rating systems reward users who are recognised as reliable workers with a higher reputational rating. These users have a privileged status on the platform itself, especially in terms of visibility. This gives them a better opportunity to be contacted by other users, which in turn has an effect on how their rewards are calculated. Ultimately this gives them power over others with lower ratings. Such tools can produce ambivalent results and may be subject to the bias of some with a fear of negative retaliation by other users. For example, in a study of BlaBlaCar, it was observed that the reputation rating played an important role in recognising legitimacy by users, but it was also clear that users gave biased ratings. More than half of users in the survey considered rating as a duty, just under half considered it a functional and practical factor, but only 0.5% considered it useless (Arcidiacono et al., 2016). However, 23% gave positive ratings only because they did not want to do wrong to the person with whom they travelled, thus confirming the presence of a positive bias in online reviews, as argued by Resnick and Zeckhauser (2002). These findings are further supported by analysis of users' comments, where the lemmas that are most often used within the textual corpus are all positive. To get to the first lemma with a negative connotation you have to go down to 93rd place, where we find *delay*, which recurs in the feedback corpus 1712 times. Negative assessments are limited overall, demonstrating a tendency not to give feedback when there is a problem. This level of satisfaction is therefore ambivalent: it testifies to the efficiency of the matching and would seem to minimise the cases of dissatisfaction. However, it also highlights how the social dimension of this service, which actively promotes a culture of sharing, effects the ratings system.

It has to be remembered that algorithmic systems are characterised by a deep opacity (Pasquale, 2015), which promote a sense of renewed individualism (Papacharissi, 2011; Hearn, 2016). It is observed by Campbell (2018), from a survey among Uber and Lyft drivers, that complaints about earnings potential had increased after the introduction of pooling services, UberPool and Lyft Line. This enlarged the degree of disaffection of these workers for this service, as pooling service algorithms were said to reduce the overall ride fares for drivers. Moreover, the rating system can stimulate a *superstar effect*, which is not evenly distributed. The only way to increase the rating is to accept the greatest number of tasks possible, which as discussed in the previous chapter, means longer driving hours and employing tactics to try and game the rating system, the workings of which can never be fully understood by drivers. This is a particular problem for Uber workers, for whom the reputational system not only acts as an enabler of transactions but is a system that regulates and organises the work of the drivers to such a degree that if their rating level falls below a certain average, they will be banned from using the platform.

Sharing mobility communities?

Notions of community do not intrinsically belong to all forms of sharing mobility. Historically, the community was a central element in the early phases of sharing mobility (see Chapter 2), in both the sharing of vehicles among students and neighbours, and in the case of slugging and casual carpooling. With the spread of sharing mobility facilitated by digital technologies, notions of community have largely disappeared in vehicle sharing and ridesharing services. As we

Figure 5.1 The characteristics of a sharing mobility community

have shown, they have remained central to peer-to-peer car-sharing and carpooling systems (although somewhat differently compared to those early experiences of sharing mobility). Nevertheless, in light of the relational dynamics observed so far, can we really say that sharing mobility ever produces true communities? If yes, what kind of community are we talking about? And what would distinguish this community from other types community? Figure 5.1 shows the characteristics that we propose define a sharing mobility community. These can be broken down as follows:

- On-life communities: it is necessary for ride-sharers to interact digitally but their needs and their relationships extend outside the platform. Following Floridi (2015), interactions do not remain confined to the online or offline sphere but are instead based on the constant interrelations between these two spheres of action.
- Openness: unlike other types of community, the exclusivity of belonging is neither an explicit nor an implicit element. On the contrary, sharing mobility services develop with the idea of an open coopetition and integration between different groups and communities, as shown by the recent tendency to develop agglomerate apps between different mobility platforms and services (i.e. Urbi, Free2Move, Moovit).

- Algorithmic rules: in the community the forms of control and homogenisation of behaviours and practices are governed by the algorithm that organises information flows and distributes them, albeit in a non-transparent manner.
- Pragmatical: unlike traditional communities anchored in places with long-held principles, such as local communities and technical-professional communities, mobility communities appear to be linked more strongly by mutual and specific mobility needs, which over time can develop strong bonds between urban commuters.
- Alone/together: the relationships between the subjects are not re-current but rather occasional and dispersed, which gives rise to a more fluid and much less binding community formation coherent with the idea of the *networked-self* (Papacharissi, 2011) when compared with traditional structures of community relations.
- On sale: since the rise of market-oriented shared mobility services, the commodification of community becomes a salient trait that shapes public and commercial rhetoric about sharing mobility, which can also be said to sublimate the motivations among the users.

In early elaborations of the concept of community, two main elements were identified:

- Communities share physical space (Parsons, 1951; Simmel, 1903; Sorokin and Zimmerman, 1929; Tönnies, 1887).
- Communities share common and implicit feelings of belonging (McIver, 1924; Weber, 1922).

In the knowledge society a third factor was then added through the conceptualisation of "community of practices" (Wenger, 1998), which refers to a domain, a repertoire of tools, methods, techniques, tricks, styles, theories, approaches, perspectives, and languages that bind a group together. In the era of digital platforms, new communities emerge, which are aggregated around new forms of identity, based on information and knowledge (i.e. professional social networks), hedonistic symbols (e.g. brand communities), or issues of global interest (i.e. Open Source community). In this sense they are not necessarily tied to territorial or cultural affiliations. Communities can escape specific locations, be wide-ranging and constituted by a weak system of reciprocity mediated by new media technologies. In the nineties, Rheingold introduced the concept of "virtual communities", defining them as "a group of people who may or may not meet one another face-to-face, and who exchange words and ideas through the mediation of computer bulletin boards and networks" (1993: 58). Whilst some of these elements remain consistent today, it might now be more appropriate to apply the concept of *augmented society* or "on life" (Floridi, 2015) because it is increasingly the case that communities are defined by shared norms and practices that unfold between online and offline arenas.

At the same time, the emotional experience of being part of a community is commodified by the platform communication strategy in order to transform the community feeling into affection for the brand. This creation of brand-communities through notions of sharing and emotional adhesion (Muniz and O'Guinn, 2001; Schouten and McAlexander, 1995) is ultimately a marketing strategy designed to increase brand equity through associations with authenticity.

In the case of sharing mobility, communities do develop in some cases, but they tend to be characterised by social homogeneity. Users tend to be young, highly educated, affluent, and more active and engaged online. At the same time, they share common interests and motivations that encourage them to exchange in a sharing economy. In specific regard to peer-to-peer carpooling, they share an asset and a commonality over how the rules for governing this sharing should be respected. We could talk about these groups as hybrid communities because interactions and experiences don't take place exclusively online or offline, but rather between these spaces (Reischauer and Mair, 2018). Setiffi and Lazzer (2018: 89) come to these conclusions in their study of BlaBlaCar, stating that:

> Although BlaBlaCar is not intended as a territorial network defined by clear boundaries, it activates relationships that are both local and repeated over time. Above all, however, it activates processes that change the relationship with the so-called "stranger".

The two Italian researchers stress that there are elements of BlaBlaCar which support a thesis of community practice, wherein formal rules, shared knowledge, shared feelings and emotions, and the collective need for transport constitute an adhesive for community building (Warde, 2014). Arcidiacono et al. (2016) similarly conclude that BlaBlaCar is a brand community *and* a community of practice. Findings from their survey suggest that BlaBlaCar users felt affection towards the brand and other users, and that users considered it an ethical responsibility to develop rituals, traditions, and codes of practice between users. Their data suggest that BlaBlaCar is the connective tissue that binds user experiences and practices both online and offline, as well as a platform that facilitates mobility exchanges. This was illustrated in the fact that almost half (44.4%) of their interviewees stated that they shared the underlying philosophy and values of the service and felt like members of a community that was contributing to positive changes in the world (e.g. in terms of managing resources and regaining trust among people). This sense of belonging is strongly influenced by the level of interaction experienced on the platform. For instance, BlaBlaCar Ambassadors have on average a much higher commitment to these values than other users. 85% of this group claimed to be very involved in the community, compared to those with a lower level of experience, where it was only 26%. In this sense, it can be said that intense use of the service increases user ranking at the same time as it develops feelings of brand loyalty and community identity. Ultimately, however, BlaBlaCar is peculiar case. In other mobility platforms, as we have demonstrated throughout this book, the community dimension can be co-opted by the commercial use of the term, which is when the concept of community is reduced to an appendix of the brand, where actors do not share a collective identity or social capital and instead operate as individuals (Schor and Attwood-Charles, 2017). BlaBlaCar could be representative of what we might call "coming communities" with an unrealised potential, as suggested by Arvidsson (2018). It could however remain undeveloped as a simple and symbolic network of people akin to other "imagined communities" identified by historical sociological analysis (see Anderson, 1983; Cohen, 1985), where the collective meaning and practices community are only loosely tied together. What is clear is that BlaBlaCar has adopted an effective marketing and communication strategy to promote and empower the idea of community, which is working to convince users that it is a legitimate community of practice in the sharing mobility sector.

From communities to cooperatives

The fear that sharing mobility services are being co-opted by financial capitalism has led to the emergence of a significant resistance movement, particularly in the US, where there have been a number of initiatives designed to offer an alternative to this scenario. This movement has come to be known as *platform cooperativsm* (Scholz and Schneider, 2017). The basic idea is to build cooperative platforms owned by the workers/users, based on open source technologies, which respect ethical working conditions and redistribute value to the users who produced it. The history of the cooperative movement can be dated back to the mid-1800s when industrial workers in Rochdale, North

England, formed a cooperative body to defend the labour rights and their families from the negative effects of the industrial revolution. During this time, specific principles were developed that the cooperative movement continues to abide by today. These are: free accession (an "open door" policy); democratic control of members ("one head, one vote"); return cap on capital; political and religious neutrality; and the development of co-operative education. Platform co-operativism, almost nostalgically, resumes the idea of the cooperative model, trying to adapt it to the new challenges of digital technology, promoting solutions that look above all at participatory governance models, user and worker responsibility, and the development of collaborative social projects. In the following, we outline cases of where the model of platform co-operativism has been adopted by sharing mobility platforms across the world.

An interesting case rooted in Canada is called *Modo*. Founded in 1997, in Vancouver, Modo had 16 initial members and 2 vehicles. This carsharing project, originated from a degree thesis, and today has more than 600 vehicles and about 20,000 users active in Vancouver, Greater Victoria, Nanaimo. In the last year the number of users has increased by 16.7% and different types of cars have been added to the fleet to satisfy a wider range of users. The Modo app allows you to find vehicles (owned by the cooperative) nearby and rent them with fixed rates on an hourly basis, differentiated by the type of user. Member-owners are shareholders of the co-op which means they get a vote in decisions made, as well as the best rates for car sharing. These members pay a registration fee of 500 Canadian dollars and get reduced rates on the services offered by the cooperative. The service is also open to external users, but 61% of its users are members of the cooperative. Over time, the business model has evolved progressively by integrating additional services such as ridesharing. Regarding the governance model, Modo is a cooperative of consumers and a social enterprise. The board of directors is composed of volunteers, which are elected from the membership base, and the paid-up share capital is fully repayable to members based on clauses of the cooperative memorandum.

Innovation in terms of business model and financial tools can be seen in the Austin based ridesharing company, Arcade City, which started out as a Facebook group called "Arcade city Austin – Request a ride" (founded by Christopher David). The business model of Arcade City is based on Ethereum cryptocurrency technology (traded as ARCD tokens). This funding system, called ICO (Initial Coin Offer), allows cooperatives to raise a large amount of capital without having to go through the rigorous and regulated process of traditional venture capital. The start-up released 100 million ARCD tokens, the primary means by which to purchase services in the Arcade City ecosystem, on the Ethereum blockchain during a 28-day campaign starting on November 1st, 2016 (84% of which were publicly available) as a means to fund the ridesharing service. Today Arcade City is active in the city of Austin, USA and in the Philippines where it has a customer base of about 70,000 active users. It uses a network of entrusted "guild leaders" (experienced drivers on the platform), who are paid with the ARCD currency, to develop the service in new markets.

A further case in Europe is Partago. This service creates collaborative networks among several cooperatives with a strategic focus on sustainability. Partago is a Flemish Electric Car Sharing coop involved in creating a European Platform Coop called *The Mobility Factory* (TMF). Each member can invest a maximum of €5,000 and all users of Partago have a vote, regardless of their financial contribution, on profit allocation, of which 5% is intended for projects to promote sustainable mobility. Since 2017, Partago has become part of a network for local electric mobility coops, which has three objectives: to use renewable energy, to build a network of mobility coops (e.g. linking SOM Mobilitat in Catalunya with renewable energy coop providers such as EnerCoop, SOMenergy, and Copernico) and to develop data/information-sharing collaborations among the providers of the network to improve the platforms involved.

Another interesting case is Ridygo, a French cooperative ridesharing platform founded in 2015, which now has 5,000 active users. One interesting aspect of this cooperative is that part of the revenue is donated to social projects that fight unemployment. Another is that the cooperative is focused on providing a service for people who live in areas with poor transport links, thus providing a means to access employment opportunities not otherwise easily available to them. The legal form adopted is that of the SCOP, a cooperative and participatory hybrid company, which according to new French legislation includes both cooperative production companies and companies of collective interest. Currently, the membership base is very restricted and limited to working members (mainly software developers), but it is the cooperative's goal to open up to user-members. Ridygo uses virtual credits worth 10 cents, each credit corresponds to 1 km travelled. Ridygo retains a 20% commission on transactions, of which 50% is used for bank transactions to support projects to combat unemployment.

In conclusion, these initiatives are characterised by localism, but also by their desire to scale differently from the prevailing capitalist platform model. They aim to do this mainly through partnerships and networks with similar operators and actors, or through alternative financial tools such as cryptocurrency and time banks to support long-term development and expansion strategies. Nevertheless, the innovativeness of these initiatives has not escaped to the attention of big players of the digital economy such as Uber and Airbnb, who have recently declared that they are considering the idea of involving their users in company ownership, confirming the tendency for capitalist actors to cannibalise any antagonistic movement. As these large companies increasingly move towards a model of public shareholders it will be interesting to see how they plan on doing this, and how the platform cooperative movement will respond.

Notes

1 www.shareable.net/.
2 https://p2pfoundation.net/.
3 www.uia-initiative.eu/en/uia-cities/turin.
4 https://platform.coop/.

6 Conclusion

The premise of sharing a ride, vehicle, or transport costs with other people has a long history. Today, new digital technologies, business models, politics, and social attitudes have meant that shared mobility has broken through as a popular means of transport. This much is obvious when we look at the data purporting to the year on year increases in market share, user numbers, and capital investments in the sector. It is also clear from the significant media attention and hype that this industry has become a part of contemporary public discourse about the sharing economy, and especially about transport technology, labour rights, and platform regulation.

The number of academic books, articles, and industry reports about shared mobility has increased alongside this rise. Indeed, there is a now a rich body of resources from which to gleam insights about how this industry has grown, what impact it is having around the world, and how it will continue to grow. Nevertheless, amongst this work is a distinct lack of sociological analysis about how and where these impacts are felt, for whom these services are, and whose interests they serve. It is in this gap that we have situated this book, as an attempt to wade through the sociological complexities that constitute and are constituted by these novel forms of technologically mediated practices of mobility.

Throughout the chapters, we have emphasised that shared mobility is not a universal, homogenous model, but rather a contextually bound practice. We have demonstrated how the specificities of space, place, culture, politics, and economics have significantly affected the ways that shared mobility services operate in the world. We have argued that local contexts make a difference to how sharing mobility services operate, who uses them, and how data is collected and operationalised through them. Even Silicon Valley services like Uber must always be situated in ways where the complex relations between the local and the global are carefully considered. By doing so, we have aimed to highlight the fragmented local realties of a burgeoning global sector, which are often in sharp contrast to the seamless experiences of on-demand mobility services that we encounter through our digital interfaces.

Highlighting just some of these "glocal" realities is the first step in deciding what kind(s) of shared mobility we want to have. From the evidence presented in this book, we argue that there is an urgent need for us to rethink shared mobility in relation to its social, economic, and environmental impacts, and its role in working towards more equitable forms of mobility justice (Sheller, 2018). Though the current state of the shared mobility sector is certainly exciting, opening up potentially revolutionary agendas for urban mobility, more must be done by technologists, regulators, policymakers, and users to consider these relational impacts, and then to develop services that actively attend to the inequalities that they can produce. We hope that readers of this book will acknowledge and act upon the inequalities posed by the status quo, which is dominated by a few global venture capital backed companies with economic rather than social aims in mind.

In this conclusion, we layout a potential pathway for shaping change in the sector, beginning with what we see as a necessary shift in business models and then discussing how guiding principles and radical changes in social and political action will be necessary.

Decentring the Silicon Valley model: from competition to cooperation

The notion that "sharing" services are inherently Silicon Valley services or Silicon Valley-inspired services needs to be decentred if we are to realise significant change in the sector. We should value other lesser known, but no less active models, which demonstrate that alternative modes of sharing mobility, and the sharing economy more broadly, are possible. This is not to say that we should reject all aspects of the Silicon Valley model, but instead to say that developing viable, sustainable, and socially responsible forms of sharing mobility will require a multimodal approach that draws from and integrates ideas from across a spectrum of models.

There is little doubt that the Silicon Valley business model has firmly put shared mobility at the centre of the public debate about urban transport. The success of this model, in terms of its popularity and global growth, can be attributed to the culture of financial backing by venture capitalists and the automotive industry, and inflated expectations of growth that prevail in Silicon Valley. This model, augmented by vast sums of marketing capital and sophisticated technological design, encourages shared mobility services to scale quickly and rapidly expand their user base. However, services using this model are increasing coming under pressure for their aggressive and misleading market strategies, (re)producing social (im)mobilities, disrupting existing transport businesses and mobility services, and flouting the rules with respect to transport regulation, worker rights, data privacy, and competition laws. These issues are fuelling a strong social and political opposition, which has compromised the reputation and development of this model over time. The opposition that Uber has faced in recent years is emblematic of this. From its beginnings as start-up that aimed to revolutionise mobility by supporting a local transport business in crisis and guaranteeing greater efficiency and flexibility, Uber has since become a highly financialised global corporation that is symbolic of the greed and unscrupulousness practices of the big players in the sharing economy. In many places around the world it is now opposed by its workers and the municipalities in which it operates. This has led Uber to expand quickly into "non-western" markets in Asia and Africa where there is a fast-growing demand for shared mobility and where the social and regulative constraints of this expansion are more relaxed.

Alternatives to the Silicon Valley model are based mainly on local mobility needs and cultures of practice that encourage elements of public participation, collaboration, and mutuality that were present in the early experiences of car-sharing mobility dating back to the late 1940s. The most significant of these models today can be found in the form of cooperative and communitarian movements, which support a participatory approach to ownership, value redistribution, and governance based on multiple stakeholder engagement from car owners, drivers, users, local municipalities, and other cooperative enterprises.

As discussed in Chapter 5, these alternative models have been successful in some cases. In particular, peer-to-peer and cooperative models represent the service with the greatest innovative potential for creating cultures of sharing mobility. This is because the advantages and positive impacts of these services are not limited to flexibility of use, convenience, or ecological impact, but also because they tend to focus on the creation of social relations and mutual trust between users. These elements could be key drivers in producing community groups based on shared values for urban citizenship. As the cooperatives discussed in this book demonstrate, these communities are more than simply "imagined communities" or "potential communities". Instead they are living communities who share values and strategies for urban well-being through their everyday practices of sharing mobility.

Nonetheless, such models have proved difficult to scale because they lack significant financial support and adequate resources, are in direct competition to dominant service providers,[1] and are contingent on the support of a cohesive and highly committed community of members, of which there are relatively few. It is not because they do not work, but because success in this sector is judged by a services' ability to scale economically and not by a services' ability to promote community values around shared mobility practices. Being situated in a world increasingly dominated by globalised shared mobility services, alternative models therefore risk remaining confined to the margins of the market or being cannibalised by global operators themselves.

Both models have advantages and limitations that must to be addressed if we are to create solutions for the pressing needs of urban mobility. The two-tiered system of local and global enterprise today will likely not be sufficient for achieving these aims because one is geared towards maximum value extraction and the other in not easily scalable. Future services, encouraged by social and political will could instead converge on a model of plurality, in which public and private services focus on developing synergies and sensible integrations in a logic of *co-opetition*. Mobility as a Service (MaaS) initiatives have begun this work but much more is needed to help integrate and balance the aims of the different models. This move towards a plurality of services could offer solutions to help curb the new oligopolies that now dominate this sector of the sharing economy and help to promote the social values of the lesser known cooperative shared mobility movement.

Useful actions of integration could include:

- The legal commitment to multimodal payment systems by transport authorities, whereby unique payment media or technology can be used to pay or access services on multiple modes of shared transportation (including public transit). This would ensure smaller and alternative models are more visible and easily integrated into a landscape dominated by shared mobility platforms. It might also mean that these services are more easily able to reach a greater critical mass of users to form the basis of sustainable sharing communities. Though this idea of multimodal payment is nothing new,[2] much more could be done to integrate a broader range of shared mobility services into these systems.
- Cross-platform promotions and joint marketing programmes to make customers more aware of the advantages of complementary services and the strengths of a diverse sharing mobility ecosystem.

- Data collaborations where data is collected and openly shared amongst partners to improve the quality of services and address the mobility needs of the community.
- Tax innovations on behalf of the user and service provider that redistribute value to provide economic support for developing alternative shared mobility eco-systems. This could help create more sustainable cooperative experiences or other alternative forms of governance and their integration in the urban mobility planning.

Mobility policy and public values for a sharing city

The role of the public actor and public values are central to the success of urban shared mobility. Without these, the potential of cities to be liveable, democratic, and sustainable spaces is at serious risk of being subsumed by the actions and values of elite private actors. With this in mind, we now turn to a set of strategies and guiding principles for shared mobility that could be adopted to put public values at the centre of urban mobility policy. These recommendations would help create the conditions of possibility for "sharing cities" that are founded primarily on the cultures, and not economics, of sharing (McLaren and Agyeman, 2015). The aim here is to lay out general approaches that could be adopted and adapted for specific localities without devaluing the importance of a contextual understanding of shared mobility discussed above.

In the following, we unpack the *Shared Mobility Principles for Liveable Cities*,[3] which were developed in 2017 by a coalition of industry, NGO and governmental partners led by Robin Chase, the founder of ZipCar. These ten principles are based around the four themes of *sustainability, inclusivity, prosperity,* and *resilience*, and are intended for policymakers and stakeholders to consider when planning for the future of shared mobility in cities. They are described in full here because of the support they have received from across the spectrum of shared mobility services, which shows that common goals can be found between different business models.[4]

1 *Plan cities and mobility together* – calls for an integrated approach that takes into account mobility needs and systems when designing and developing the urban environment for sustainable futures.

  This approach, often labelled as "joined-up thinking" is becoming more popular with planners as they realise the relational impacts of sustainable urban development. We welcome this but would urge planners to take a broad approach to mobility and

urban design; to recognise and account for the range of (im)mobilities that new services create.
2 *Prioritise the movement of people over vehicles* – calls for planners to start with the mobility needs of urban citizens rather than single passenger polluting vehicles.

This will require a significant social, political, and economic shift in how we relate to the car as a primary means of transport. Car culture is firmly embedded in society and it will take time and a willingness for change at multiple scales for this principle to be realised.
3 *Support the efficient use of space and shared vehicles* – calls for local and regional government to play a fundamental role in managing the efficient use of vehicles and street space.

Shared mobility services have begun to offer pooling options and some significant steps have been taken to provide parking spaces for shared vehicles. Nevertheless, some form of regulation and incentive will be necessary to encourage governments and service providers to make these more widely available.
4 *Engage stakeholders through the transition to shared mobility* – calls for multilateral governance practices that meaningfully engage stakeholders in decision-making at all stages of the transition process. This refers not only to the design phase, but also to its implementation, management, and legacy phases.

Multilateral planning and public-private governance have the potential to make heard the voices of those that are often neglected in urban mobility planning. Key to this strategy will be true collaboration rather than the faux sincerity for "local issues" that has become characteristic of such public-partnerships. The value of these voices must be acknowledged and acted upon if we are to create shared mobility services that serve to address the inequalities of urban mobility. In particular, much more attention should be paid to the voices and practices of those that are subject to digital divides and those that live in shared mobility deserts.
5 *Design equitable services* – calls for shared mobility design that is equitable and accessible for everyone by default, regardless of age, gender, race, ethnicity, income, ability, or any other identifying characteristics.

This principle gets to the heart of what we mean when we say that citizens should have a right to shared mobility in the city. Managing and innovating urban mobility does not only mean acting on the articulation of the available transport networks. By designing equality into systems, and leaving open the opportunity for recursive changes after implementation, shared mobility providers can help to avoid developing innovations that only benefit the lives of mobile elites. Preventing shared mobility from becoming an elitist phenomenon is of paramount importance if we are to realise its revolutionary potential.

To add further to this principle, we would also urge policymakers and stakeholders to consider other material socio-cognitive and cultural factors when designing equitable systems for the future. These include:

- *Digital literacy* – knowledge of how to use these services should not be assumed. Educational programmes that teach people how to use these services and what impacts they can have to everyday mobilities should be made available, particularly for elderly populations.
- *Inclusive representational practices* – the importance of inclusive marketing and media practices that reflect the true realities of urban cultures should not be underestimated nor ignored.
- *Spatial distribution of services* – the geographies of, and proximities to, available shared services should be carefully considered to reflect all socio-economic characteristics. Significant attention should be placed on improving the current state of shared mobility deserts.
- *Fair pricing in non-central areas* – users should not be penalised in their use of shared mobility services for living away from city centres. Shared mobility services should recognise and accommodate for the fact that not everyone can or wants to live in city centres.
- *Subsidised pricing* – certain categories of users, including those on low or no incomes should have trip costs subsidised in some capacity.
- *Rethinking ratings* – current systems designed to be opaque to anyone but the platform gamify shared mobility and create spaces of surveillance that help platforms avoid taking responsibility for their part in the transaction. This create anxieties for both drivers and passenger and disrupts the conditions for the possibility of shared mobility communities and culture.

Designing equitable services also means guaranteeing employment rights for those that work in the sector. The platform economy is the latest expression of the global economy and has become illustrative of the complexities of work in a post-industrial digital era. The tendency to generate more and more non-standard contractual activities that remain outside traditional forms of employment protections should be challenged. Shared mobility services can provide opportunities for inclusion in an increasingly unstable market, but more needs to be done to give equitable legal rights to workers that are clearly employees. The casual contractor model popularised by Silicon Valley platforms leads to regressive forms of labour protection, broken career paths, increased individualisation, and social marginalisation. Service providers and policymakers should recognise that it is their responsibility to change this damaging practice when designing services for the future.

6 *Transition towards zero emissions* – calls for shared mobility to be an instrument and symbol of environmental sustainability by adopting low and no emissions vehicles.

Although the data does not certify homogeneous results, the studies identified in this book show that shared mobility services are already moving in a positive direction here. Nevertheless, more should be done to increase the pace of change, especially if we are to achieve the global target of a 45% reduction in carbon emissions by 2030 recommended by the recent IPCC (2018) report on climate change. Simply put, this means vehicles shared mobility services must implement strict electric or zero emissions policies over the next 5–10 years, and related infrastructures must be installed to make this achievable.

7 *Seek fair user fees* – calls for shared mobility to pay a fee for its impact on society, road and street infrastructure, congestion, and pollution in the city.

On the face of it, fair user fees are important because they put the onus on shared mobility services to take some responsibility for the impacts they have on cities. However, such fees should be carefully designed in order to avoid exclusionary practices. The most widespread of fees used to manage shared mobility services today are spatialised; focused on providing incentives or sanctions to encourage drivers to stay in or out of specific urban spaces (e.g. city centre congestion zones and low emission zones), or to permit or prevent access and use of specific urban infrastructures (e.g. shared car parking spaces and electric vehicle charging points). Whilst these measures do have some positive impacts such as improving air quality and walkability in city centres, we should be weary that they can also create new barriers to mobility in terms of cost, access and proximity to shared mobility services as well as having the potential to simply push the problems of congestion and air quality into the urban suburbs. Future incentives should therefore take into account the *capabilities* of people and how they are diversely distributed in the urban environment, and not only focus on urban centres.

8 *Deliver public benefits via open data* – calls for shared mobility services to adopt open and interoperable data policies where anonymised data is made available for use in urban planning and design.

This principle addresses the datification practices that are intrinsic to the shared economy. As discussed in this book, data are central to how these new mobility enterprises operate. We argue that urban mobility data should not be the exclusive property of a single provider. Following Van Dijck et al. (2018), it's time to stimulate a serious debate around the public value and ownership of mobility data that moves us away from the misguided assumption that data should always be the property of service providers. The majority of users are still in the dark over how algorithmic systems govern the functioning of shared mobility platforms, particularly in regard to how these systems mediate the matching and distribution of incentives and rewards among users. Initiatives such as open data city portals, which are increasingly widespread in cities like London, Stockholm, and New York and the policies of "open architecture", in which code and data are made openly available to workers/members in some cooperatives are welcomed in this regard. Nevertheless, simply making data available does not go far enough. Services and policymakers need to develop practices that identify and guarantee data privacy standards, create codes of conduct that prevent data misuse, and educate the public on how mobility data can be used. Data policies such as these could encourage more equitable practices in the planning, design, and management of these services.

9 *Promote integration and seamless connectivity* – calls for shared mobility services to integrate with other transit services, payment systems, and transport hubs.

This principle follows the intentions of the MaaS paradigm, which are to create a multimodal and technologically integrated system of mobility across cities, regions, and even countries. To achieve this goal, there will need to be a radical step change in how we conceptualise mobility, and service providers will need to be willing to work with other providers, as well as local and national governments.

10 *Automated vehicles must be shared* – calls for shared mobility to adopt a principle of equity and inclusivity when rolling out automated vehicles.

This last principle refers to the future of shared mobility and suggests that automated vehicles in cities must be shared if we hope to create equitable forms of mobility. Without making efforts to design equality into the development of these systems, we run the risk of reproducing the inequalities of our existing car culture. We are still some way off the full implementation of automated systems, so we urge designers and policymakers not to focus too much on speculative future-thinking, and instead focus on addressing the more pressing equity issues of shared mobility that exist today.

These ten principles offer a good starting point for decision makers and stakeholders interested in designing more socially and sustainably just shared mobility services. Nevertheless, despite being supported and recognised as important considerations by numerous well-known service providers (including Didi, BlaBlaCar, Uber, Lime, Lyft, Ola, Ofo, and Zipcar), NGOs and government departments, none of these principles is yet to be legally binding in any meaningful way. This poses a familiar problem encountered elsewhere in response to well-intended guiding principles devised in other sectors (e.g. Fair Trade), which is that they are not enforceable by law leaving those that break their commitment to these principles with little accountability.

What we require is a radical rethinking of the current shared mobility sector that is supported by effective and recursive legislation, where we see sharing mobility primarily as a right and not a market. This could mean:

- Designing shared mobility as a public service that is integrated into existing public transit systems. This will require significant political will by central and local governments, especially in countries which have favoured the privatisation of transportation services in recent decades.
- Lobbying central and local governments to enshrine these principles in law and hand out significant sanctions for those services found to be in breach of these commitments.
- Creating effective public-private partnerships where significant and legally binding commitments are made to engage with a range

of stakeholders at all levels. As we've discussed, these partnerships are one of the more popular means of addressing the issues raised by sharing mobility, but far more attention is need on creating meaningful partnerships.
- Creating independent regulatory bodies made of a diverse group of stakeholders ((im)mobility researchers, community members, and platform workers as well as urban planners, policymakers, and platform designers) with real legal power to govern shared mobility and its relational impacts.
- Incentivising communities, companies, and institutions that are not part of the mobility industry to sign up and invest in these principles.

What next for sharing mobility?

The future of sharing mobility is not fixed; there is room for change, but this change will only come about with fundamental shifts in social and political attitudes. Central to these shifts is the understanding of and commitment to mobility justice and relational thinking on the issue of sharing mobility. As we've argued in this book, sharing mobility is an issue tied to many of the important issues of our day (e.g. labour, social life, climate change, as well as transport and mobility) and needs to be designed, governed, and used with these relations in mind.

For those of us examining the impacts and potential of shared mobility, there is still much more work to be done. This book only begins to scratch the surface on who is using these services, how and why they're being used, what social and environmental impacts they are having, and how they might be designed and governed in the future. To end this book, we suggest four areas that we see as needing further attention when researching and teaching shared mobility as a relational issue. These are by no means exhaustive, but they offer a starting point for future investigation and pedagogy. We should:

1. Pay particular attention to the voices and practices of sharing mobility in non-western contexts, where we are seeing the largest growth in the sector. As we mentioned above, we need to decentre the notion that shared mobility is a Silicon Valley phenomenon in order to understand more about how sharing mobility plays out in different global contexts. This could help us develop a more holistic understanding of what sharing mobility is and what it means to different people and places, which in turn could be used to foster multi-lateral, rather than top-down, design practices where services are developed with cultures of mobility in mind.

2 Examine further the diversity of public values held by shared mobility users (drivers, riders, and passengers) and non-users. What is it that users and non-users want from these services and where do they see their responsibility in working towards just shared mobilities? Whilst the full weight of responsibility should not fall on the shoulders of users, more could be done to explore and test what motives users to participate in the sharing economy, what users would be willing to adapt to, and what it would take for non-users to adopt sharing mobility practices.
3 Examine the potential of social and environmental scoring schemes in order to test their acceptance and impact in the shared mobility sector by service providers, policymakers and users. We should address the questions of who will give out these scores, what will determine these scores and how such scores can be used to force meaningful change? Innovative pilot projects such as those set up by the Fair Work Foundation to score on-demand work platforms provide a template from which shared mobility scoring and labelling might build on.[5]
4 Develop multi-level educational programmes that outline the impacts and potential of sharing mobility, and how it relates to the broader issues of mobility justice. The programmes should focus on the many advantages of sharing mobility modes compared to other mobility options, and educate people on the potential of these modes in fostering meaningful community practices.

Notes

1 As Borowiak (2019) has observed in relation to Uber and the Alliance Taxi Cooperative in Philadelphia, cooperative car sharing movements can be crushed by the weight of evasive regulatory practices and market disruptions caused by dominant platforms.
2 See for example the Citymapper Pass and the recent discussions around multimodal ticketing in the EU (https://ec.europa.eu/transport/themes/logistics/events/2018-year-multimodality-travel-information-planning-and-ticketing_en).
3 www.sharedmobilityprinciples.org/.
4 These are by no means the only guiding principles for more just shared mobilities or sharing economies. See for example, Scholz (2016).
5 See https://fair.work.

Bibliography

Ademe, (2015a), Etude nationale sur le covoiturage de courte distance, enquêtes auprès des utilisateurs des aires de covoiturage, available at: www.ademe.fr/enquete-aupres-utilisateurs-covoiturage-longue-distance

Ademe, (2015b), *Etude nationale sur le covoiturage de courte distance, approche méthodologique d'évaluation de l'impact du covoiturage sur les polluants atmosphériques et le CO_2*, Paris: Agence de l'environnement et de la maîtrise de l'énergie.

Agatz N., Erera A., Savelsbergh M., and Wang X., (2012), 'Optimization for dynamic ride-sharing: A review', *European Journal of Operational Research* 223: 295–303.

Ainge Roy E., (2019), 'Lime e-scooters temporarily banned in two New Zealand cities'. *The Guardian*, 25th February 2019, available at: www.theguardian.com/world/2019/feb/25/lime-e-scooters-temporarily-banned-in-two-new-zealand-cities

Altimeter, (2013), *The Collaborative Economy*, San Mateo American Cities, available at: http://innovativemobility.org/wpcontent/uploads/2016/07/Impactsofcar2go_FiveCities_2016.pdf

Amey A.M., Attanucci J., and Mishalani R., (2011), 'Real-time ridesharing: Opportunities and challenges in using mobile phone technology to improve rideshare services', *Transportation Research Record: Journal of the Transportation Research Board* 2217: 103–110.

Anderson B., (1983), *Imagined Communities*, London: Verso.

Anderson D.N., (2016), 'Wheels in the head: Ridesharing as monitored performance', *Surveillance & Society* 14(2): 240–258.

Andreotti A., Anselmi G., Eichhorn T., Hoffmann C.P., Jürss S., and Micheli M., (2017), 'Participation in the sharing economy: European perspectives', Report from the EU H2020 Research Project Ps2Share, available at: www.bi.edu/globalassets/forskning/h2020/participation-working-paper-final-version-for-web.pdf

Angel S., (2011), *Making Room for a Planet of Cities*, available at: www.lincolninst.edu/sites/default/files/pubfiles/making-room-for-a-planet-of-cities-full_0.pdf

Bibliography

APTA, (2016), *Shared Mobility and the Transformation of Public Transit*, available at: www.apta.com/resources/reportsandpublications/Documents/APTA-Shared-Mobility.pdf

Arcidiacono D., (2013), *Consumatori Attivi. Scelte d'Acquisto e Partecipazione per una Nuova Etica Economica*, Milano: Franco Angeli.

Arcidiacono D., (2017a), 'Innovare la mobilità urbana attraverso la condivisione', in Lodigiani R. (ed.), *La città dell'innovazione*, Milano: Franco Angeli.

Arcidiacono D., (2017b), 'Start up ed economia collaborativa: forme alternative di scambio economico o mito della disintermediazione?', *Quaderni di Sociologia* 73(1): 29–47.

Arcidiacono D., (2018), 'Contesto italiano e benchmarking nazionale', in LAMA e Ministero per lo sviluppo economico (ed.), *Share Your Move Urban Smart Mobility & Platform Coop*, Roma: Studio di fattibilità, pp. 1–20.

Arcidiacono D., Mainieri M., and Pais I., (2016), *Quando la sharing economy fa innovazione sociale*, Milan: Sharitaly.

Arcidiacono D., and Pais I., (2018), 'Think mobility over: A survey on Car2go users in Milan', in Bruglieri M. (ed.), *Multi-disciplinary Design of Sharing Services*, London: Springer.

Arcidiacono D., and Podda A., (2017), 'Sharing time: new forms of reciprocity in the digital economy', *Work Organisation Labour & Globalisation* 11(2): 39–57.

Armstrong H., Gorst C., and Rae J., (2019), *Renewing Regulation: Anticipatory Regulation in an Age of Disruption*, London: Nesta.

Arvidsson A., (2018), 'Value and virtue in the sharing economy', *The Sociological Review* 66(2): 289–301.

Arvidsson A., Caliandro A., Cossu A., Deka M., Gandini A., Luise V., Orria B., and Anselmi G., (2016), 'Commons based peer production in the information economy', Research Report, P2Pvalue Project, available at: https://p2pvalue.eu/wpcontent/uploads/2013/07/Deliverable_4.3.1.pdf

Attoh K.A., (2011), 'What kind of right is the right to the city?', *Progress in Human Geography* 35(5): 669–685.

Ayuntamiento de Sevilla, (2010), *Estudio sobre el uso de la bicicleta en la ciudad de Sevilla*, Sevilla: Gerencia de Urbanismo.

Balaram B., (2016), *Fair Share: Reclaiming Power in the Sharing Economy*, London: RSA.

Baptista P., Melo S., and Rolim C., (2014), 'Energy, environmental and mobility impacts of car-sharing systems: Empirical results from Lisbon, Portugal', *Procedia – Social and Behavioural Sciences* 111: 28–37.

Bardhi F., and Eckhardt G.M., (2012), 'Access-based consumption: The case of car sharing', *Journal of Consumer Research* 39(4): 881–898.

Beer D., (2018), *The Data Gaze*, London: Sage.

Belk R., (2007), 'Why not share rather than own?', *Annals of the American Academy of Political and Social Science* 611: 126–140.

Bibliography 113

Belk R., (2014), 'Sharing versus pseudo-sharing in Web 2.0', *Anthropologist* 18(1): 7–23.

Benkler Y., (2004), 'Sharing nicely: On shareable goods and the emergence of sharing as a modality of economic production', *Yale Law Journal* 114: 273–358.

Bennett W.L., and Segerberg A., (2012), 'The logic of connective action: Information', *Communication & Society* 15(5): 739–768.

Berger G., Feindt P., Holden E., and Rubik F., (2014), 'Sustainable mobility: Challenges for a complex transition', *Journal of Environmental Policy & Planning* 16(3): 303–320.

Berger T., Frey C.B., Levin G., and Danda S.R., (2018), *Uber Happy? Work and Well-being in the "Gig Economy"*, Paper presented at the 68th Economic Policy Panel Meeting, Vienna, 4–5th October 2018.

Bhuiyan J., and Warzel C., (2014), '"God view": Uber investigates its top New York executive for privacy violations', *BuzzFeed News*, 18th November 2014, available at: www.buzzfeednews.com/article/johanabhuiyan/uber-is-investigating-its-top-new-york-executive-for-privacy#.rdGYbpymz

Bingham-Hall J., (2016), *Future of Cities: Commoning and Collective Approaches to Urban Space*, London: Government Office for Science.

Bliss S., (2019), 'Uber was supposed to be our public transit', *Citylab*, 29th April 2019, available at: www.citylab.com/transportation/2019/04/innisfil-transit-ride-hailing-bus-public-transportation-uber/588154/

Blumenberg E., and Smart M., (2014), 'Brother can you spare a ride? Carpooling in immigrant neighbourhoods', *Urban Studies* 51(9): 1871–1890.

Böker L., and Meelen T., (2017), 'Sharing for people, planet or profit? Analysing motivations for intended sharing economy participation', *Environmental Innovation and Societal Transitions* 23: 28–39.

Boltanski L., and Chiappello E., (1999), *Le nouvel esprit du capitalism*, Paris: Gallimard.

Borowiak C., (2019), 'Poverty in transit: Uber, taxi Coops, and the struggle over Philadelphia's transportation economy', Antipode (online), doi:10.1111/anti.12543

Botsman R., and Rogers R., (2010), *What's Mine Is Yours: The Rise of Collaborative Consumption*, London: Harper Business.

Bowcott O., (2017), 'Uber to face stricter EU regulation after ECJ rules it is transport firm', *The Guardian*, 20th December 2017, available at: www.theguardian.com/technology/2017/dec/20/uber-european-court-of-justice-ruling-barcelona-taxi-drivers-ecj-eu

Briggs M., (2014), 'Car-sharing in London: Vision 2020', *Frost and Sullivan Report*, available at: www.zipcar.co.uk/london-vision

Brommelstroet M., Nikolaeva A., Glaser M., Nicolaisen M., and Chan C., (2017), 'Travelling together alone and alone together: Mobility and potential exposure to diversity', *Applied Mobilities* 2(1): 1–15.

Bruglieri M. (ed.), (2018), *Multidisciplinary Design of Sharing Services*, London: Springer.

Bruns A., (2008), *Blogs, Wikipedia, Second Life and Beyond: From Production to Produsage*, New York: Lang Publishing.

Burris M.W., and Winn J.R., (2006), 'Slugging in Houston–Casual carpool passenger characteristics', *Journal of Public Transportation* 9(5): 23–40.

Callon M., (1998). *The Law of the Market*, Oxford: Blackwell Publisher.

Calo R., and Rosenblat A., (2017), 'The taking economy: Uber, information, and power', *Columbia Law Review* 117: 1623–1690.

Campbell H., (2018), *The Rideshare Guy 2018 Survey*, available at: www.therideshareguy.com

Canales D., Bouton S., Trimble E., Thayne J., Da Silva L., Shastry S., Knupfer S., and Powell M., (2017), *Connected Urban Growth: Public-Private Collaborations for Transforming Urban Mobility. Coalition for Urban Transitions. London and Washington, DC*, available at: http://newclimateeconomy.net/content/cities-working-papers

Cao D., (2016), 'Regulation through deregulation: Sharing economy companies gaining legitimacy by circumventing traditional frameworks', *Hastings Law Journal* 68: 1085–1110.

Carplus, (2015), *Monitoring Car Clubs. Carplus Car Club Annual Members Survey Report 2014/2015*, London.

Castells M., (1989), *The Informational City: Information Technology, Economic Restructuring, and the Urban Regional Process*, Cambridge: Blackwell.

CEC, (2011), *White Paper. Roadmap to a Single European Transport Area – Towards a Competitive and Resource Efficient Transport System*, COM (2011) 144 final, Brussels.

Cervero R., (2003), 'City CarShare: First-year travel demand impacts', *Transportation Research Record* 1839: 159–166.

Cervero R., Golub A., and Nee B., (2006), 'City CarShare: Longer-term travel demand and car ownership impacts', Working Paper 2006–07, Institute of Urban and Regional Development.

Cervero R., and Arrington G. B., (2008), 'Vehicle trip reduction impacts of transit-oriented housing', *Journal of Public Transportation* 11(3): 1–15.

CGDD, (2016). *Covoiturage longue distance: état des lieux et potentiel de croissance. Etudes & Documents du Commissariat Général au Développement Durable*, no. 146, May, available at: http://temis.documentation.developpement-durable.gouv.fr/document.html?id=Temis-0084251

Chan N.D., and Shaheen S.A., (2012), 'Ridesharing in North America: Past, present, and future', *Transport Reviews* 32(1): 93–112.

Chan N.K., (2019), 'The rating game: The discipline of Uber's user-generated ratings', *Surveillance & Society* 17(1/2): 183–190.

Chatterton P., (2018), *Unlocking Sustainable Cities: A Manifesto for Real Change*, London: Pluto Press.

Chen J.Y., (2018), 'Thrown under the bus and outrunning it! The logic of Didi and taxi drivers' labour and activism in the on-demand economy', *New Media & Society* 20(8): 2691–2711.

China Council for International Cooperation on Environment and Development, (2017), 'Sharing economy: A new economic revolution led by lifestyles', available at: https://environmental-partnership.org/wp-content/uploads/2017/08/CCICED-Sharing-Economy-A-New-Economic-Revolution-Led-by-Lifestyles.pdf

Ciari F., and Becker H., (2017), 'How disruptive can shared mobility be? A scenario-based evaluation of shared mobility systems implemented at large scale', in Meyer G., and Shaheen S. (eds.), *Disrupting Mobility, Impacts of Sharing Economy and Innovative Transportation on Cities*, London: Springer, 51–63.

City of Bremen, (2005), *Ergebnisse des Bremer Modellprojekts "Mobilpunkt". Ansätze für Car-Sharing im öffentlichen Raum*, Bremen.

Clark J., and Curl A., (2016), 'Bicycle and car share schemes as inclusive modes of travel? A socio-spatial analysis in Glasgow, UK', *Social Inclusion* 4: 83–99.

Clewlow R., and Gouri S.M., (2017), *Disruptive Transportation: The Adoption, Utilization, and Impacts of Ride-Hailing in the United States. Institute of Transportation Studies*, University of California, Davis, Research Report UCD-ITS-RR-17-07, available at: https://trid.trb.org/view/1485471

Clewlow R., and Mishra G., (2017), *Disruptive Transportation: The Adoption, Utilization, and Impacts of Ride-Hailing in the United States*. Institute of Transportation Studies, University of California, Research Report UCD-ITS-RR-17-07, Berkeley.

Cohen A., (1985), *The Symbolic Construction of Community*, Chichester: Ellis Horwood.

Cohen B., and Kietzmann J., (2014), 'Ride on! Mobility business models for the sharing economy', *Organization & Environment* 27(3): 279–296.

Cohen M., and Sundararajan A., (2017), 'Self-regulation and innovation in the peer-to-peer sharing economy', *University of Chicago Law Review* 82: 116–133.

Cohen M.J., (2012), 'The future of automobile society: A socio-technical transitions perspective', *Technology Analysis and Strategic Management* 24(4): 377–390.

Coleman J.S., (1988), 'Social capital in the creation of human capital', *The American Journal of Sociology* 94: 95–120.

Cresswell T., (2010), 'Towards a politics of mobility', *Environment and Planning D: Society and Space* 28: 17–31.

Daconto L., (2017), 'Mobilità quotidiana e inclusione nel lavoro: sfida dell'accessibilità e politiche urbane', in Bidussa D., and Polizzi E. (eds.), *Agenda Milano. Ricerche e pratiche per una città inclusiva*, Milano: Fondazione Feltrinelli EPub.

Darido G., (2016), 'Sao Paulo's innovative proposal to regulate shared mobility by pricing vehicle use', *Transport for Development World Bank blog*, available at: http://blogs.worldbank.org/transport/sao-paulo-s-innovative-proposal-regulate-shared-mobility-pricing-vehicle-use

Darido G., Torres-Montoya M., and Shomik M., (2009), *Urban Transport and CO_2 Emissions: Some Evidence from Chinese Cities*, Washington, DC: World Bank.

Bibliography

De Certau M., (1998), *The Practice of Everyday Life*, Minneapolis: Minnesota Press.

Degryse C., (2016), *Digitalisation of the Economy and Its Impact on Labour Markets* (No. 2), Brussels: ETUI.

Douglass M., and Friedmann J., (1997), *Cities for Citizens: Planning and the Rise of Civil Society in a Global Age*, Hoboken: John Wiley and Sons.

Dubois E.A., Schor J., and Carfagna L., (2014), 'New cultures of connection in a Boston Time Bank', in Schor J.B., and Thompson C.J. (eds.), *Sustainable Lifestyles and the Quest for Plenitude: Case Studies of the New Economy*, New Haven: Yale University Press.

Dunca N., (2015), 'In first, Uber to share ride data with Boston', *The Boston Globe*, 13th January 2015, available at: www.bostonglobe.com/business/2015/01/13/uber-share-ridership-data-with-boston/4Klo40KZREtQ7jkoaZjoNN/story.html

Dutzik T., Inglis J., and Baxandall P., (2014), *Millennials in Motion Changing Travel Habits of Young Americans and the Implications for Public Policy*, U.S. PIRG Education Fund Frontier Group, available at: https://uspirg.org/sites/pirg/files/reports/Millennials%20in%20Motion%20USPIRG.pdf

Ede S., (2018), 'Mobility', in Shareable (ed.). *Sharing Cities: Activating the Urban Commons*, Mountain View, CA: Shareable.

Edelman B., De Luca M., and Svirsky D., (2017), 'Racial discrimination in the sharing economy: Evidence from a field experiment', *American Economic Journal: Applied Economics* 9(2): 1–22.

Edelman B., and Luca M., (2014), 'Digital discrimination: The case of Airbnb.com', Working Paper 14–054, available at: www.hbs.edu/faculty/Publication%20Files/Airbnb_92dd6086-6e46-4eaf-9cea-60fe5ba3c596.pdf

Eisenmeier S.R.J., (2018), *Ridesharing Platforms in Developing Countries: Effects and Implications in Mexico City.* Pathways for Prosperity Commission Background Paper Series; no. 3. Oxford. United Kingdom, available at: https://pathwayscommission.bsg.ox.ac.uk/sites/default/files/2018-10/eisenmeier_ridesharing.pdf

Engels B., and Liu G.J., (2011), 'Social exclusion location and transport disadvantage amongst non-driving seniors in a Melbourne municipality', *Australia Journal of Transport Geography* 19(4): 984–996.

Eurobarometer, (2016), *Collaborative Platform 438*, available at: http://ec.europa.eu/COMMFrontOffice/publicopinion/

Fainstein S., (2001), 'Competitiveness, cohesion and governance: Their implications for social justice', *International Journal of Urban and Regional Research* 25: 884–888.

Farajallah M., Hammond R.G., and Pénard T., (2016), 'What drives pricing behavior in peer-to-peer markets? Evidence from the Carsharing Platform BlaBlaCar. Evidence from the Carsharing Platform Blablacar', *Economics Working Paper Archive (University of Rennes 1 & University of Caen) from Center for Research in Economics and Management (CREM)*, available at: https://econpapers.repec.org/paper/tutcremwp/2016-12.htm

Farrell D., Greig F., and Hamoudi A., (2018), *The Online Platform Economy in 2018: Drivers, Workers, Sellers, and Lessors*, New York: JPMorgan Chase Institute.

Federal Highway Administration (2018), *Shared Mobility. Current practices and guiding principles, U.S. Department of Transportation*, Washington DC: FHA.

Fenton A., (2013), *Making Markets Personal: Exploring Market Construction at the Micro Level in the Car-sharing and Time Bank Markets*, Cambridge: Harvard University Press.

Ferguson E., (1997), 'The rise and fall of the American carpool: 1970–1990', *Transportation* 24(4): 349–376.

Floridi L., (2015), *The Online Manifesto: Being Human in a Hyperconnected Era*, Springer: London.

Frenken K., Meelen T., Arets M., and Van de Glind P., (2015), 'Smarter regulation for the sharing economy', *The Guardian*, 20th May.

Frenken K., and Schor J., (2017), 'Putting the sharing economy into perspective', *Environmental Innovation and Societal Transitions* 23: 3–10.

Frost and Sullivan, (2016), *Evolution of Mobility. New Business Models and Impact on the Value Chain*, available at: www.mobility-future.com/uploads/Presentations/kaushik%20madhavan.pdf

Fukuyama F., (1995), *Trust: The Social Virtues and the Creation of Prosperity*, New York: Free Press.

Furuhata M., Dessouky M. Ordóñez F., Brunet M.E., Wang X., and Koenig S., (2013), 'Ridesharing: The state-of-the-art and future directions', *Transportation Research* 57: 28–46.

Fuster Morell M., and Espelt R., (2018), 'A framework for assessing democratic qualities in collaborative economy platforms: Analysis of 10 cases in Barcelona', *Urban Science* 61: 1–13.

Gandini A., (2018), 'Labour process theory and the gig economy', *Human Relations*, online first: doi:10.1177/0018726718790002.

Gansky L., (2006), *The Mesh. Why the Future of Business is Sharing*, Penguin: New York.

Gartman D., (2004), 'Three ages of the automobile: The cultural logics of the car', *Theory, Culture and Society* 21(4/5): 169–195.

Gavin K., Bennett A., Auchincloss A.H., and Katenta A., (2016), 'A brief study exploring social equity within bicycle share programs', *Transportation Letters* 8: 177–180.

Ge Y., Knittel C.R., MacKenzie D., and Zoepf S., (2016), 'Racial and gender discrimination in transportation network companies', *National Bureau of Economic Research*, working paper: 22776.

Gleave S.D., (2018), *Carplus Annual Survey of Car Clubs: Scotland. Car Plus Report*, available at: https://como.org.uk/wp-content/uploads/2018/06/Carplus-Annual-Survey-2017-18-Scotland-Final.pdf

Global e-Sustainability Initiative (2008), *SMART 2020: Enabling the Low Carbon Economy in the Information Age*, Washington: United States Report.

Goldman Sachs, (2017), *Rethink Mobility: The 'Pay-as-You-Go' Car: Ride Hailing just the Start*, available at: https://orfe.princeton.edu/~alaink/SmartDrivingCars/PDFs/Rethinking%20Mobility_GoldmanSachsMay2017.pdf

Graham S., (2001), *Splintering Urbanism: Networked Infrastructures, Technological Mobilities and the Urban Condition*, Abingdon: Routledge.

Graham S., (2016), *Vertical City*, London: Verso.

Granovetter M., (1985), 'Economic action and social structure: The problem of embeddedness', *American Journal of Sociology* 91(3): 481–510.

Haefeli U., Matti D., Schreyer C., and Maibach M., (2006), *Evaluation Car-Sharing*. Schlussbericht, Bern: Federal Office for Energy (Eds.).

Haenfler R., Aenfler B.J., and Jones E., (2012), 'Lifestyle movements: Exploring the intersection of lifestyle and social movements', *Social Movement Studies* 1: 1–20.

Handke V., and Jonuschat H. (eds.), (2013), *Flexible Ridesharing: New Opportunities and Service Concepts for Sustainable Mobility*, Berlin: Springer-Verlag.

Harvey D., (1990), *The Condition of Postmodernity*, Cambridge: Blackwell.

Harvey D., (2013), *Rebel Cities: from the Right to the City to Urban Revolution*, London: Verso.

Hearn A., (2016), 'Structuring feeling: Web 2.0, online ranking and rating, and the digital "reputation" economy', *Ephemera. Theory & Politics in Organization* 10(3/4): 421–438.

Heinrichs H., (2013), 'Sharing economy: A potential new pathway to sustainability', *Gaia* 22(4): 228–231.

Hensley R., Padhi A., and Salazar J., (2017), *Cracks in the Ridesharing Market and How to Fill Them*, available at: www.mckinsey.com/industries/automotive-and-assembly/our-insights/cracks-in-the-ridesharing-market-and-how-to-fill-them

Hickman R., Smith D., Moser D., Schaufler C., and Vecia G., (2017), *Why the Automobile Has No Future a Global Impact Analysis*, Greenpeace Report, available at: www.greenpeace.de/sites/www.greenpeace.de/files/publications/170911_f_studie_whytheautomobilehasnofuture_final.pdf

Hiscock R., Macintyre S., Kearns A., and Ellaway E., (2002), 'Means of transport and ontological security: Do cars provide psycho-social benefits to their users?', *Transport Research* 7: 119–135.

Hochschild A.R., (1983), *The Managed Heart: The Commercialization of Feeling*, Berkeley: University of California Press.

Hoffman L. Bensinger G., and Farrell M., (2018), *Uber Proposals Value Company at $120 Billion in a Possible IPO*. The Wall Street Journal, available at: www.wsj.com/articles/uber-proposals-value-company-at-120-billion-in-a-possible-ipo-1539690343

Hui Y., Wang W., Ding W., and Liu Y., (2017), 'Behavior patterns of long-term car-sharing users in China', *Transportation Research Procedia* 25: 4662–4678.

Iacovini C., (2014), *Car Sharing. Come la sharing economy cambia la nostra mobilità*, Milano: Edizioni Ambiente.

IEA, (2009), *Transport, Energy and CO_2. Moving Toward Sustainability*. International Energy Agency, Paris.
IEA, (2012). *Energy Technology Perspectives 2012. Pathways to a Clean Energy System*. International Energy Agency, Paris.
Institute for Sustainable Future, (2017), *The Sharing Economy in Developing Countries-Full Report*, Sydney.
IPCC, (2018), *Global warming of 1.5c. IPCC Report*, available at: https://report.ipcc.ch/sr15/pdf/sr15_spm_final.pdf
Jensen O.B., (2009), 'Flows of meaning, cultures of movements: Urban mobility as meaningful everyday life practice', *Mobilities* 4(1): 139–158.
Jensen O.B., Sheller M., and Wind S., (2014), 'Together and apart: Ambiences and negotiation in families' everyday life and mobility', *Mobilities* 10(3): 363–382.
Johal S., and Zon N., (2015), *Policymaking for the Sharing Economy: Beyond Whack-a-Mole*, Toronto: Mowat Centre.
JoJob, (2016), *Osservatorio Car-pooling Aziendale-Full Report*, Torino.
Kamargianni M., and Matyas M., (2017), 'The business ecosystem of mobility as a service', 96th Transportation Research Board (TRB) Annual Meeting, Washington, DC, 8–12 January, available at: http://discovery.ucl.ac.uk/10037890/1/a2135d_445259f704474f0f8116ccb625bdf7f8.pdf
Katrini E., (2018), 'Sharing culture: On definitions, values and emergence', *The Sociological Review* 66(2): 425–446.
Keeney T., (2017), Mobility as a service: Why self-driving cars could change everything, ARK Invest Research, available at: http://research.ark-invest.com/hubfs/1_Download_Files_ARK-Invest/White_Papers/Self-Driving-Cars_ARK-Invest-WP.pdf
Kelley K.L., (2007), 'Casual carpooling enhanced', *Journal of Public Transportation* 10(4): 119–130.
Kenney M., and Zysman J., (2016), 'The rise of the platform economy', *Issues in Science and Technology* 32(3), available at: http://issues.org/32-3/the-rise-of-the-platform-economy/
Kitchin R., (2014), *The Data Revolution*, London: Sage.
Kitchin R., Lauriault T.P., and McArdle G., (2017), *Data and the City*, Abingdon: Routledge.
Kitchin R., and Perng S., (2016), *Code and the City*, Abingdon: Routledge.
Kopp J., Gerike R., and Axhausen K.W., (2015), 'Do sharing people behave differently? An empirical evaluation of the distinctive mobility patterns of free-floating car-sharing members', *Transportation* 42: 449–469.
Lane C., (2005), 'PhillyCarShare: First-year social and mobility impacts of car-sharing in Philadelphia, Pennsylvania', *Transportation Research Record* 1927: 158–166.
Lane C., Zeng H., Dhingra C., and Carrigan A., (2015), 'Carsharing: A vehicle for sustainable mobility in emerging markets', *World Resources Institute Ross Centre for Sustainable Cities*, available at: https://wricitieshub.org/publications/carsharing-vehicle-sustainable-mobility-emerging-markets
Latour B., (2005), *Reassembling the Social: An Introduction to Actor Network Theory*, Oxford: Oxford University Press.

Leadbeater C., and Miller P., (2014), *The Pro-am Revolution*, available at: www.demos.co.uk/files/proamrevolutionfinal.pdf

Leenes R., van Brakel R., Gutwirth S., and De Hert P., (2018). *Data Protection and Privacy: (In)visibilities and Infrastructures*, New York: Springer.

Lefebvre H., (1968), *Le droit á la ville*, Paris: Anthropos.

Leszczynski A., (2016), 'Speculative futures: Cities, data, and governance beyond smart urbanism', *Environment and Planning A* 48(9): 1691–1708.

Li Y., and Voege T., 'Mobility as a Service (MaaS): Challenges of implementation and policy required', *Journal of Transportation Technologies* 7: 95–10.

Little A., (2015), *The Future of Urban Mobility 2.0: Towards Networked, Multimodal Cities of 2050*. International Association of Public Transport (UITP), available at: www.uitp.org/sites/default/files/members/140124%20Arthur%20D.%20Little%20%26%20UITP_Future%20of%20Urban%20Mobility%202%200_Full%20study.pdf

Lloyd's, (2018), Innovation report 2018-sharing risks, sharing rewards: Who should bear the risk in the sharing economy?, available at: www.lloyds.com/.../risk.../2018/sharing-risks-sharing-rewards.pdf

Lucas K., (2012), 'Transport and social exclusion: Where are we now?', *Transport Policy* 20: 105–113.

Lucas K., Mattioli G., Verlinghieri E., and Guzman A., (2016), 'Transport poverty and its adverse social consequences', *Proceedings of the Institution of Civil Engineers – Transport* 169(6): 353–365.

Maertins C., (2006), Die intermodalen Dienste der Bahn: Mehr Mobilität und weniger \ Verkehr? Wirkun-gen und Potenziale neuer Verkehrsdienstleistungen. Discussion Paper SP III – available at: www.ssoar.info/ssoar/handle/document/11384

Manzella F., Sundurarajan A., (2016), *Entering the Trust Age*, Paris: BlaBlaCar & NYU-Stern.

MAPC, (2018), *Fare Choices. A Survey of Ride-Hailing Passengers in Metro-Boston*, available at: www.mapc.org/wp-content/uploads/2018/02/Fare-Choices-MAPC.pdf

Martin C.J., (2016), 'The sharing economy: A pathway to sustainability or a nightmarish form of neoliberal capitalism?', *Ecological Economics* 121: 149–159.

Martin E., and Shaheen S., (2016), Impacts of car2go on vehicle ownership, modal shift, vehicle miles traveled, and greenhouse gas emissions: An analysis of five north American Cities, Berkeley's Transportation Sustainability Research Center (TSRC), available at: http://innovativemobility.org/wp-content/uploads/2016/07/Impactsofcar2go_FiveCities_2016.pdf

Martin E., Shaheen S., and Lidicker J., (2010), 'Impact of car-sharing on household vehicle holdings: Results from a North American shared-use vehicle survey', *Journal of the Transportation Research Board*, 2143: 150–178.

Martin E.W., and Shaheen S.A., (2011), 'Greenhouse gas emission impacts of carsharing in North America', *IEEE Transactions on Intelligent Transportation Systems* 12(4): 1074–1086.

Mass Transit Rider Research Report, (2018), *Key Factors Influencing Ridership in North America. The Emerging Urban Mobility Ecosystem*. Full Report, available at: http://info.masabi.com/mass-transit-rider-research-report-2018-key-factors-influencing-ridership-in-north-america

Mateo-Babiano I., (2015), 'Public bicycle sharing in Asian Cities', *Journal of the Eastern Asia Society for Transportation Studies* 11: 60–74.

Mauss M., (1924), 'Essai sur le don. Forme et raison de l'échange dans les sociétés primitives', *in L'Année sociologique*, Paris: Felix Alcan (English translation: *The Gift*, London: Routledge, 1990).

Mazzella F., and Sundararajan A., (2016), *Entering the Trust Age*, Paris: BlaBlaCar & NYU-Stern.

McCarthy T., (2007), *Auto Mania: Cars Consumers and the Environment*, New Haven: Yale University Press.

McCraw T.K., (2010), *Prophet of Innovation: Joseph Schumpeter and Creative Destruction*, Boston: Belknap Press of Harvard University Press.

McIver R. M., (1924), *Community*, London: Macmillan.

McLaren D., and Agyeman J., (2015). *Sharing Cities: A Case for Truly Smart and Sustainable Cities*, Cambridge, MA: MIT Press.

Meryll-Linch and Bank of America, (2018), *BofAML Autos: Mobility as a Service. Will the Car Has a Future*, available at: www.maas-market.com/sites/default/files/MARTYN%20BRIGGS_0.pdf

Meyer G., and Shaheen S. (eds.), (2017), *Disrupting Mobility, Impacts of Sharing Economy and Innovative Transportation on Cities*, London: Springer.

Middleton J., (2018), 'The socialities of everyday urban walking and the "right to the city"', *Urban Studies* 55(2): 296–315.

Miller D., (ed.), (2001), *Car Culture*, New York: Berg.

Miller S.R., (2015), 'First principles for regulating the sharing economy', *Harvard Journal on Legislation* 53(1): 147–202.

Mishkin L., (2018), 'Growth and earnings in the "online platform economy": A comment on the new JPMorgan Chase Institute study', *Uber Under the Hood Blog*, available at: https://medium.com/uber-under-the-hood/growth-and-earnings-in-the-online-platform-economy-a-comment-on-the-new-jpmorgan-chase-institute-501ef491cce8

MIT, (2017), *Platform Strategy Summit-Report*, Cambridge, MA: MIT Press.

Mitchell D., (2003), *The Right to the City: Social Justice and the Fight for Public Space*, New York: Guilford Press.

Moeller S., and Wittkowski K., (2010), 'The burdens of ownership: Reasons for preferring renting', *Managing Service Quality: An International Journal* 20(2): 176–191.

Muñiz A., and O'Guinn T., (2001), 'Brand community', *Journal of Consumer Research* 27(4): 412–432.

Murphy E. and Usher J., (2015), 'The role of bicycle-sharing in the city: Analysis of the Irish experience', *International Journal of Sustainable Transportation* 9(2): 116–125.

Myers D., and Cairns S., (2009), *Carplus Annual Survey of Car Clubs*, available at: https://trl.co.uk/sites/default/files/PPR399.pdf

Navigant Research, (2018), *Mobility as a Service. The Future of Moving People: Carsharing, Ride-Hailing, Micro Transit, Automated Mobility, and P2P Rental Services - Full Report*, Chicago.

Nelissen R.M.A., and Meijers M.H.C., (2011), 'Social benefits of luxury brands as costly signals of wealth and status', *Evolution and Human Behavior* 32(5): 343–355.

Nesta, (2014), *Making Sense of the Collaborative Economy in UK-Final Report*, London.

Nielsen, (2013), *Global Survey on Share Communities*, Report, www.nielsen.com/content/dam/nielsenglobal/apac/docs/reports/2014/Nielsen-Global-Share-Community-Report.pdf

Nijland H., and Meerkewk J.V., (2017), 'Mobility and environmental impacts of car sharing in the Netherlands', *Environmental Innovation and Societal Transitions* 23: 84–91.

Nikolaeva A., Adey P., Cresswell T., Lee J.Y., Nóvoa A., and Temenos C., (2019), 'Commoning mobility: Towards a new politics of mobility transitions', *Transactions for the Institute of British Geographers*, doi: 10.1111/tran.12287.

Nooren P., van Gorp N., van Eijk N., and Ó Fathaigh R., (2018), 'Should we regulate digital platforms? A new framework for evaluating policy options', *Policy & Internet* 10(3): 264–301.

Novaco R.W., and Collier C., (1994), 'Commuting stress, ridesharing, and gender: Analyses from the 1993 State of the commute study in Southern California', Working Paper UCTC No. 208, University of California Transportation Center, Berkeley.

NYLPI, (2018), 'Left behind: New York's for-hire vehicle industry continues to exclude people with disabilities', *NYLPI Report*, available at: https://nylpi.org/nylpi-report-reveals-accessible-transportation-failures-of-uber-and-lyft/

Observatorie de la Confiance, (2014), *La confiance en commun*, Paris: LE Groupe La Poste.

OECD, (2006), *Decoupling the Environmental Impacts from Transport from Economic Growth*, OECD: Paris.

ONSM, (2016), *Osservatorio nazionale sulla Sharing Mobility-I Rapporto La Sharing Mobility in Italia: numeri, fatti e potenzialità*, available at: http://osservatoriosharingmobility.it/cover-galleries/

Owyang J., (2014), *Sharing is the New Buying: How to Win in the Collaborative Economy*, New York: Crowd Companies.

Owyang J., and Samuel A., (2015), *The new rules of collaborative economy*, New York: Crowd Companies.

Pais I., and Del Maral L., (2018), 'Feminization of Labor, defeminization of Time Banks: Digital time banking and unpaid virtual work', *International Journal of Media and Cultural Politics* 14(1): 55–75.

Pais I., and Provasi G., (2015), 'Sharing economy: A step towards "re-embedding" the economy?', *Stato e Mercato* 105(3): 347–377.

Pankratz D.M., Nuttal K., Eggers W.D., and Turley M., (2018), *Regulating the Future of Mobility: Nalancing Innovation and the Public Good in Autonomous Vehicles, Shared Mobility, and Beyond*, London: Deloitte Center for Government Insights.

Papacharissi Z. (ed.), (2011), *A Networked Self: Identity, Community, and Culture on Social Network Sites*, Abingdon: Routledge.

Parigi P., and State B., (2014), 'Disenchanting the world: The impact of technology on relationships', *Social Informatics* 8851: 166–182.

Parsons T., (1951), *The Social System*, Abingdon: Routledge.

Pasquale F., (2015), *The Black Box Society: The Secret Algorithms that Control Money and Information*, Boston: Harvard University Press.

PEW, (2016), *Gig Work, On Line Selling and Home Sharing*. Full Report, available at: www.pewinternet.org/2016/11/17/gig-work-online-selling-and-home-sharing/

Polanyi K., (1957), 'The Economy as Instituted Process', in Polanyi K., Arensberg C.M., and Pearson H.W. (eds.), *Trade and Market in the Early Empires: Economies in History and Theory*, New York: Free Press.

Price J., DeMaio P., and Hamilton C., (2006). *Arlington Carshare Program: 2006 Report*.

Purcell M., (2002), 'Excavating Lefebvre: The right to the city and its urban politics of the inhabitant', *GeoJournal* 58(2–3): 99–108.

PWC (2015), *Sharing Economy*. Consumer Intelligence Series, available at: www.pwc.fr/fr/assets/files/pdf/2015/05/pwc_etude_sharing_economy.pdf

Reich R., (2015), *Saving Capitalism: For the Many, Not the Few*, New York: Knopf.

Reinghold A., (1993), 'A slice of life in my virtual community', in Harasim L.M. (ed.), *Global Networks, Computers and International Communication*, New York: The MIT Press.

Reischauer G., and Mair J., (2018), 'Platform organizing in the new digital economy: Revisiting online communities and strategic responses. Research', *Sociology of Organizations*, 57: 113–135.

Research and Markets Report, (2018), *Mobility as a Service (MaaS) Market 2025-Global Analysis and Forecasts by Service Type, Application Platform, Business Model & Vehicle Type*.

Resnick P., and Zeckhauser R., (2002), 'Trust among strangers in internet transactions: Empirical analysis of ebay's reputation system', in Michael R., and Baye M.R. (eds.), *The Economics of the Internet and E-Commerce*, Amsterdam: Elsevier Science.

Rifkin J., (2014), *Zero Marginal Cost Society*, London: Griffin.

Rode P., Floater G., Thomopoulos N., Docherty J., Schwinger P., Mahendra A., and Fang W., (2017), 'Accessibility in Cities: Transport and Urban Form' in Meyer G., and Shaheen S. (eds.), *Disrupting Mobility, Impacts of Sharing Economy and Innovative Transportation on Cities*, London: Springer.

Roland Berger, (2017a), *Industry 4.0 and India's Automotive Industry*, http://assocham.tv/static.assocham.tv/upload/product1/1499410952.pdf

Roland Berger, (2017b), *Think: Act. Car-sharing in China*, Munich.

Rosenblat A., (2018), *Uberland: How Algorithms Are Rewriting the Rules of Work*, Berkley: University of California Press.

Rosenblat A., Levy K., Barocas S., and Hwang T., (2016), 'Discriminating tastes: Uber's customer ratings as vehicles for workplace discrimination', *Policy and Internet* 9(3): 256–279.

Rosenblat A., and Stark L., (2016), 'Algorithmic labor and information asymmetries: A case study of Uber's drivers', *International Journal of Communication* 10: 3758–3784.

Rubin O., (2015), 'Contact between parents and adult children: The role of time constraints, commuting and automobility', *Journal of Transport Geography* 49: 76–84.

Rydén C., and Morin E., (2005) *Mobility services for urban sustainability: Environmental assessment 2005*. Bremen.

Schaefers T., (2013), 'Exploring carsharing usage motives: A hierarchical means-end chain analysis', *Transport Research Part A* 47: 69–77.

Schaller B., (2018), 'The new automobility: Lyft, Uber and the future of American cities', *Schaller Consulting*, available at: www.schallerconsult.com/rideservices/automobility.html

Schaller Consulting, (2018), *The New Automobility: Lyft, Uber and the Future of American Cities*, available at: www.schallerconsult.com/rideservices/automobility.pdf

Scheiber N., (2017), 'How Uber uses psychological tricks to push its drivers' buttons', *The New York Times*, 2nd April 2017, available at: www.nytimes.com/interactive/2017/04/02/technology/uber-drivers-psychological-tricks.html

Scholz T., (2016), *Platform Cooperativism: Challenging the Corporate Sharing Economy*, New York: The Rosa Luxemburg Foundation.

Scholz T., and Schneider N. (eds.), (2017), *Ours to Hack and to Own: The Rise of Platform Cooperativism, a New Vision for the Future of Work and a Fairer Internet*, New York: OR books.

Schor J.B., (2014), 'Debating the sharing economy. Great Transition Initiative', available at: www.greattransition.org/

Schor J.B., and Attwood-Charles W., (2017), 'The "sharing" economy: Labor, inequality, and social connection on for-profit platforms', *Sociology Compass* 11(8): e12493.

Schor J.B., Attwood-Charles W., Cansoy M., Ladegaard I., and Wengronowitz R., (2018), *Dependence and Precarity in the Sharing Economy*, available at: https://cirhr.library.utoronto.ca/sites/cirhr-edit.library.utoronto.ca/files/sefton_lectures/seftonwilliamslecture_4th_2018_schor.pdf

Schor J.B., and Fitzmaurice C.J., (2015), 'Collaborating and connecting: The emergence of the sharing economy', in Reisch L., and Thogersen J. (eds.), *Handbook on Research on Sustainable Consumption*, Cheltenham: Edward Elgar.

Schouten J.W., and McAlexander J., (1995), 'Subcultures of consumption: An ethnography of the new bikers', *Journal of Consumer Research* 22: 43–61.

Schüll N., (2012), *Addiction by Design: Machine Gambling in Las Vegas*, Princeton, NJ: Princeton University Press.

Scialpi R., (2018), *La crisi del bike sharing asiatico. Le novità di quello europeo, Milano compresa*, available at: www.touringclub.it/notizie-di-viaggio/la-crisi-del-bike-sharing-asiatico-e-le-novita-di-quello-europeo-milano-compresa

Setiffi F., and Lazzer G.P., (2018), 'Riding free riders? A study of the phenomenon of BlaBlaCar in Italy', in Cruz I., Ganga R., and Wahlen S. (eds.), *Contemporary Collaborative Consumption. Trust and Reciprocity Revisited*, Verlag: Springer.

Shaheen S., Bell C., Cohen A., and Yelchuru B., (2017), 'Travel behaviour: Shared mobility and transportation equity, *U.S. Department of Transportation Report*, available at: www.fhwa.dot.gov/policy/otps/shared_use_mobility_equity_final.pdf

Shaheen S.A., Cohen A., and Chung M.S., (2009), 'North American Carsharing: 10-Year Retrospective ', *Transportation Research Record: Journal of the Transportation Research Board* 2011: 35–44.

Shaheen S., and Cohen A., (2008), 'Worldwide car-sharing growth: An international comparison', *Transportation Research Record: Journal of the Transportation Research Board* 1992: 81–89.

Shaheen S., and Cohen P., (2007), 'Growth in worldwide sharing car sharing: An international comparison', *Journal of Transportation Research Board*, 1992: 81–89.

Shaheen S., Cohen P., and Zohdy I., (2016), 'Sharing mobility: Current practices and guiding principles', *U.S. Department of Transportation Report*, available at: www.ops.fhwa.dot.gov/publications/fhwahop16022/fhwahop16022.pdf

Shaheen S., Elliot W., Martin A., Cohen R., and Finson S., (2012), *Public Bikesharing in North America: Early Operator and User Understanding*, San Josè: Mineta Transportation Institute.

Shaheen S., Sperling D., and Wagner C., (1998), 'Car-sharing in Europe and North America: Past, present, and future', *Transportation Quarterly* 52(3): 35–52.

Shaheen S.A., Cohen A., and Roberts J.D., (2006), 'Carsharing in North America: Market growth, current developments and future potentials', *Transportation Research Record: Journal of the Transportation Research Board* 1986: 116–124.

Shareable, (2018), *Sharing Cities: Activating the Urban Commons*, Mountain View, CA: Shareable.

Shaw J., and Graham M., (2017), *Our Digital Rights to the City*, BY-NC-SA: Meatspace Press.

Sheller M., (2018), *Mobility Justice: The Politics of Movement in an Age of Extremes*, London: Verso.

Sheller M., and Urry J., (2006), 'The new mobilities paradigm', *Environment and Planning A: Economy and Space* 38(2): 207–226.

Simmel G. (1903), *Die Grosstädte und das Geistesleben*, Dresden: Petermann.

Simmel G., (1950), *The Sociology of George Simmel*, New York: The Free Press.

Sioui L., Morency C., and Trépanier M., (2012), 'How carsharing affects the travel behavior of households: A Case Study of Montréal, Canada', *International Journal of Sustainable Transportation* 7(2): 52–69.

Sivak M., and Schoettle B., (2012), 'Recent changes in the age composition of drivers in 15 countries', *Traffic Injury Prevention* 13(2): 126–132.

Slee T., (2017), *What's Yours Is Mine: Against the Sharing Economy*, New York: Or Books LLC.

Söderström T.P., and Klauser F., (2014), 'Smart cities as corporate storytelling', *City* 18(3): 307–320.

Sorokin P., and Zimmerman C.C., (1929), *Principles of Rural-Urban Sociology*, New York: Henry Holt and Company.

Srnicek N., (2016), *Platform Capitalism*, London: Polity Press.

Stark D., (1996), 'Heterarchy: Asset ambiguity, organisational innovation and the post-socialist firm', CAHRS Working papers, 21: 1–39.

Stark D., and Watkins E.A., (2018), 'The möbius organisational form: Make, buy, cooperate, or coo-opt?', *Sociologica* 12(1): 65–80.

Statista, (2018), *Digital Market Outlook*, available at: www.statista.com/outlook/digital-markets

Steenhoven J., Burale I., Toye V., and Buré C., (2016), *Shifting Perspectives: Redesigning Regulation for the Sharing Economy*, Toronto: MaRS Solution Lab.

Stocker A., Lazarus J., Becker D. and Shaheen S., (2016), 'Effects on vehicle use and ownership, travel behavior, quality of life, and environmental impacts', *Berkeley's Transportation Sustainability Research Center* (TSRC), available at: http://innovativemobility.org/wp-content/uploads/Zipcar-College-Market-Study-2015.pdf

Stokes K., Clarence E., Anderson S., and Rinnie A., (2014), *Making Sense of the Collaborative Economy in the UK*, London: Nesta.

SUMC, (2016), *Shared Mobility and the Transformation of Public Transit*, Research Analysis for the American Public Transportation Association. TCRP Report 188 Pre-Publication Draft, available at: www.tcrponline.org/PDFDocuments/tcrp_rpt_188.pdf

Sundararajan A., (2016), *The Sharing Economy: The End of Employment and the Rise of Crowd-Based Capitalism*, Cambridge, MA: MIT Press.

Susha I., Janssen M., and Verhulst S., (2017), 'Data collaboratives as a new frontier of cross-sector partnerships in the age of open data: Taxonomy development', *Proceedings of the 50th Hawaii International Conference on System Sciences, in Waikoloa, Hawaii* (2691–2700).

Swiss Federal Statistical Office, (2017), *Population's Transport Behavior 2015*, Neuchâtel.

Täuscher K., and Kietzmann J., (2017), 'Learning from failures in the sharing economy', *Management Information Systems Quarterly Executive* 16(4): 253–263.

TCRP, (2016), Car-sharing: Where and how it succeeds, available at: www.trb.org/Publications/Blurbs/156496.aspx

TFL, (2018), *Policy Statement: Private Hire Services in London. Transport for London*, available at: http://content.tfl.gov.uk/private-hire-policy-statement.pdf

Toffler A., (1980), *The Third Wave*, New York: Bantam.

Tönnies F., (1887), *Gemeinschaft und Gesellschaft*, Leipzig: Buske.
TransitCenter, (2014), *Who's on Board? 2014 Mobility Attitudes Survey*, available at: http://transitcenter.org/publications/whos-on-board-2014/#download-report
TSRC, (2015), *Car-sharing for Business|Zipcar Case Study & Impact Analysis*, available at: http://innovativemobility.org/wp-content/uploads/2015/07/Zipcar_Corporate_Final_v6.pdf
Uber, (2019), *NYC update – Uber*, available at: www.uber.com/drive/new-york/resources/driving-hour-limits/
UIC, (2016), 'Status of the competition for long distance trips at the aggregated level. Carpooling, bus, train, private car and air competition on long distance trip', Toulouse.
Uitermark J., Nicholls W., and Loopmans M., (2012), 'Cities and social movements: Theorizing beyond the right to the city', *Environment and Planning A: Economy and Space* 44(11): 2546–2554.
ULI, (2013), ULI Survey on Housing, Transportation and Community, available at: https://americas.uli.org/research/centers-initiatives/terwilliger-center-for-housing/research/community-survey/
United Nations, (2017), Desa – Population Division – World Population Prospects, available at: www.un.org/development/desa/capacity-development/tools/category/demographic-analysis-population/
Urry J., (2000), *Sociology beyond Society, Mobilities for the 21st Century*, London: Routledge.
Urry J., (2004), 'The "System" of Automobility', *Theory, Culture & Society* 21(4–5): 25–39.
Vaccaro A., (2016), 'Highly touted Boston-Uber partnership has not lived up to hype so far'. *The Boston Globe*, 16th June 2016, available at: www.boston.com/news/business/2016/06/16/bostons-uber-partnership-has-not-lived-up-to-promise
Van Dijck J., Poell T., and De Waal M., (2018), *The Platform Society*, New York: Oxford University Press.
Verlinghieria E., and Venturini F., (2018), 'Exploring the right to mobility through the 2013 mobilizations in Rio de Janeiro', *Journal of Transport Geography* 67: 126–136.
Viechnicki P., Khuperkar A., Fishman T.D., and Eggers W.D., (2015), *Sharing Mobility: Reducing Congestion, and Fostering Faster, Greener, and Cheaper Transportation Options*, London: Deloitte University Press.
Walsh D., (2017), 'Dilemma for Uber and Rival: Egypt's demand for data on riders', *The New York Times*, 10th June 2017, available at: www.nytimes.com/2017/06/10/world/middleeast/egypt-uber-sisi-surveillance-repression-careem.html
Warde A., (2014), 'After taste: Culture, consumption and theories of practice', *Journal of Consumer Culture* 14(3): 279–303.
Weber M., (1922), *Wirtschaft und Gesellschaft*, Tubingen: Mohr.
Weick K.E., (1988), 'Enacted sensemaking in crisis situations', *Journal of Management Studies* 25: 305–317.

Wells P., and Beynon M.J., (2011), 'Corruption, automobility cultures, and road traffic deaths: The perfect storm in rapidly motorizing countries?', *Environment and Planning* 43: 2492–2503.

Wells P.E., and Dimitrios X., (2015), 'From "freedom of the open road" to "cocooning": Understanding resistance to change in personal private automobility', *Environmental Innovation and Societal Transitions* 16: 106–119.

Wenger E., (1998), *Communities of Practice: Learning, Meaning and Identity*, New York: Cambridge University Press.

Wilhelms M., Henkel S., and Falk T., (2016), 'To earn is not enough: A means-end analysis to uncover peer-providers' participation motives in peer-to-peer car-sharing', *Technological Forecasting and Social Change* 125: 38–47.

Witt A., Suzor N.P., and Patrik W., (2015), 'Regulating ridesharing in the peer economy', *Communication Research & Practice* 1(2): 174–190.

World Bank, (2014). *Supporting Reports II – Urban China*, Washington, DC.

Zeng H., and Lane C., (2015), *Car-sharing in Hangzhou CHINA: A Focus Group Study*, available at: https://wrirosscities.org/sites/default/files/Embarq_CarsharingChina_final_print.pdf

Zou M., (2017), 'The regulatory challenges of "uberization" in China: Classifying ride-hailing drivers', *International Journal of Comparative Labour Law and Industrial Relations* 33(2): 269–294.

Index

Note: Page numbers followed by "n" denote endnotes.

accessibility 10, 16, 44, 71, 80, 85
Africa 13, 26–27, 39n1, 100
algorithm 2, 11, 19, 54–61, 65–69, 74, 86, 89–92, 106
Amsterdam 9, 21–22, 59
artificial intelligence 24–25, 65
app 2, 7, 16–18, 21, 40, 58–64, 91, 95
Arcade City 95–96
Arcidiacono D. 4, 33, 39, 47, 82–83, 89, 93; and Pais I. 35–37, 48, 81–82; and Podda A. 79
Arvidsson A. 94
Asia 3, 13, 26–28, 32, 48, 58, 100; Asian market 28–29; Asian cities 14, 22, 29
Auckland 54
Austin 51, 59, 60, 95–96
Australia 14, 61
automotive 14–18, 21, 24–26, 29, 99

Barcelona 36, 38, 53
Belgium 17, 30, 34
bike sharing 3, 7, 8, 11, 18, 22–23, 29–32, 36–38, 54, 57, 60, 81
BlaBlaCar xi, 4, 7, 19, 23, 28–30, 35, 39, 60, 82–84, 87–99
Bogotá 67
Boston 20, 38, 67–68, 85
Brazil 14, 39n2, 61
Bremen 34
Bulgaria 54
business angels 26

Cairo 53
Calgary 34
California 23, 57, 70, 84
Canada 3, 17, 52n2, 76n8, 95
capitalism 4, 7, 9–10, 55, 79, 94
Car2go 17, 29, 31–34, 37, 48, 81–82
Careem 20, 67
car culture 13, 51, 103, 107
carpooling 6–8, 19–23, 28–30, 38–39, 47–48, 60, 82, 84–87, 90, 93
car sharing 7, 17–22, 24–40, 42, 44–51, 81, 91, 95–96, 100, 109; co-operative 17, 51
Chase, R. 21, 102
China 3, 14–18, 22, 27–32, 37, 57–58
CityMapper 69, 109n2
city: smart 42, 72; sharing 42, 102
civic spaces 43
civil society 10
climate change 15, 105, 108
co-opetition 101
Co-Wheels 17–18, 51
collaborative economy 1–3, 5
commoning 51, 69
community ix, 2–5, 11, 17–24, 30, 41–45, 49–51, 71, 78, 80–94, 100, 109
competition: laws 100; market 23, 34, 53, 101
congestion ix, 9, 16–18, 38, 48, 54–58, 71–74, 105–106; *see also* traffic
COOP taxi 51
cooperative 4, 17, 79, 94–97, 100–102, 106

Index

data: broker 58; ethics 67; financial 67; location 58, 66; open 102, 106; privacy 54, 56, 67, 100, 106; regulation 56, 66–69
datafication 68
de Blasio, B. 59, 66
de-motorisation 14–16
#DeleteUber 51, 75
Delhi 53, 59
delivery 16, 21, 33
Denmark 17, 29, 54
deregulation 56
Didi 4, 7, 30, 58, 107
digital: divides 44, 46–47, 103 (*see also* participation divides); interfaces 62, 74, 89, 99; literacy 104; payment systems 22, 46, 87
dockless bike-sharing 32
driverless technology 21, 25
Dunedin 54

Egypt 67, 76n13
emissions viii–x, 14–15, 38–39, 45, 50, 52, 55, 70–74, 105; *see also* pollution
employment 8, 47, 51, 55–56, 60–62, 65–66, 73–74, 96; *see also* labour
environment 15, 21, 31–35, 39–42, 45, 48–55, 60, 72–80, 91, 102–109
Ethiopia 57
Europe 3–4, 17–23, 27–32, 36–39, 48, 96; European market 3, 38–39; European cities 14, 20, 29; European Commission 2, 15

Facebook 69, 83, 88, 95
Fair Work Foundation 75, 109
feedback 84, 88, 90
France 3, 17–22, 26–31, 34, 61, 84
free-floating 17, 22, 32, 34, 37

gamification 62
GDPR 68
gender 2, 41, 47, 64, 84, 103
Germany 14, 17–18, 29, 32, 35–36
gig: economy 2, 60, 75; work 61, 66
Go-Jek 58
Google 58
governance: multilateral 103; platform 4, 53; public-private 103

Grab 23, 27, 58
Granovetter M. 78
green-washing 75

health x, 54, 58
homophily 79, 84–86
HOV 23
Hungary 54

imagined communities 94, 100
impact viii, ix, 2, 5, 8, 13, 24, 32–34, 36–45, 49–50, 53–58, 63–66, 69, 72–75, 85–88, 98–100, 104–109
India 14, 23, 29–30, 37, 58
Indonesia 24, 58
infrastructure 6, 24–25, 32, 41, 50, 68, 73, 105
innovation xi, 5–11, 13, 20, 27, 34, 53–55, 69, 95, 102, 104
inter-modality 10, 36, 39
investors 29–31, 33, 71, 87
IOT 16, 25
IPO 33, 52
Italy 8, 14, 17–18, 29–35, 47, 84

Japan 17, 29
Juno 61

Kigali 51, 57

labour: practices 53–54, 56, 60, 70, 75; rights 58–60, 73–74, 95, 98; surveillance 64
Latin America 26
Lefebvre H. 9, 42–43, 52n1
licensing 54
Lime 7, 54, 67, 107
Lisbon 67
littering 54, 60
lobbying 56, 59, 70, 75, 107
London 9, 10, 14, 18, 22, 29, 32, 36–38, 45–46, 52, 56, 59, 62–64, 67–69, 106
Lyft 7, 11, 20, 30, 32–33, 36, 49, 59–61, 70, 85–86, 90, 107

McLaren D. and Agyeman J. 9, 42, 51, 61, 62, 85, 95, 102
Malaysia 27, 58
Manzella F. and Sundurarajan A. 88

Index

marketing 46–47, 50, 70, 93–94, 100–101, 104
Martin E. 10, 36–37
micro transit 4, 17, 20
Milan 9, 31–32, 34, 48, 81, 83
minimum wage 63
mobility as a service 6–8, 26, 101
mobility: injustice 46, 55, 69, 74; deserts 103–104; Justice x, 11, 40–41, 43, 45, 51, 54–55, 66, 69, 72–75, 99, 108–109
Modo 95
Montreal 35

network effects 58
New York 20–21, 29, 38, 49, 52–53, 59, 61, 63, 66, 73, 106
Nice 67
North America 3, 7, 14, 19, 23, 28, 32, 39; cities 34, 36, 37; market 31–32

Ofo 7, 22, 107
Ola 7, 23, 30, 33, 58, 107
open source 2, 92, 94
ownership x, 18, 37, 45–46, 48, 51–52, 100, and data 67, 106

Paris 14, 22, 29, 32, 36–38, 43, 53, 84
Partago 96
participation divides 46–47; *see also* digital divides
peer-to-peer 18–21, 33, 39, 69–70, 81, 91, 93
platform viii–ix, 1–12, 16, 20–21, 30, 38, 48, 51–77, 79, 82–92, 94–98, 101, 104–109
Poland 29, 54
Polanyi K. 78, 80
pollution ix–x, 9, 15, 18, 38, 45, 105; *see also* emissions
post-automobility 14
price gouging 66
pricing: subsidised 104; surge 60, 65–66, 74
Private Hire Vehicles 74
prosumer 1, 4
pseudo-sharing 44–45, 50–51
public-private partnerships 67, 70, 72, 103, 107

race 2, 41, 64, 79, 103
rating system 63–65, 70, 85, 89–90, 104
reciprocity 9, 18, 80, 86, 92
redistribution 2, 80, 86, 100
regulation 5, 10, 11, 14, 22–23, 33–34, 53–77, 85, 98, 100, 103
relationality 11, 86
revenues 7, 28–29, 33, 66, 96
Ride-hailing ix, 31, 86
Ride-sharing 19–24, 28–32, 36, 39–41, 46, 48, 51–75, 80, 85–86, 90, 96
RideAustin 51, 60
Ridygo 96
Rosenblat A. 41, 61, 64, 76, 85; and Calo R. 62, 85; and Stark L. 61
Rwanda 24, 57

SafeMoto 24, 50, 57
safety: driver 49, 59, 70, 75; passenger 49, 53–54, 70, 75
San Francisco 6, 9, 20–23, 34, 38
Sao Paulo 53, 73
Schor J., viii–x, 1, 56, 60, 78, 85, 94
scooter x, 4–5, 7, 16–17, 54, 60
Scotland 18, 51
Seoul 9, 51
Shaheen S. 8, 10, 21, 41, 46–48
Shareable 50, 55, 79
sharing economy viii, 1–5, 10–12, 29–30, 42, 46, 49, 53, 56, 60, 66, 67, 71, 78–80, 88, 93, 99–101
Silicon Valley 8, 59, 98–100, 105, 108
Singapore 22, 27, 32, 54
social networks 6, 83–84, 88, 92, 105
stakeholders 56, 71, 102–104, 107–108
start-up 18, 25–28, 34, 39, 96, 100
station-based 16–17, 32, 34, 36
Stockholm 106
sustainability 5–10, 26, 31, 34–41, 48–51, 96, 102, 109
Sweden 34

taxi xi, 7, 20, 23–24, 27, 29, 34, 36, 51, 54, 57, 59, 60, 66, 74
Texas 59
traffic ix, 8–9, 16, 18, 29, 34–38, 50–52, 58, 74; *see also* congestion
transit deserts 74

transport: equity 54, 60; exclusion 9, 44; poverty 44
transportation network companies 57, 72
trust 87–89, 96, 100

Uber 1, 4, 7, 10–12, 20–21, 27, 32–36, 39–40, 49, 52, 56–79, 85–86, 90, 92–97, 99, 102
urban planning 9, 67, 80, 102–103, 106

Vancouver 34
vehicle sharing 16–18, 28, 33, 81, 86, 90
venture capital 60, 79, 96, 99
Virginia 6, 57

Washington 34

Zipcar 7, 17, 21, 36, 40, 45–46, 102, 107

For Product Safety Concerns and Information please contact our EU representative GPSR@taylorandfrancis.com
Taylor & Francis Verlag GmbH, Kaufingerstraße 24, 80331 München, Germany

www.ingramcontent.com/pod-product-compliance
Lightning Source LLC
Chambersburg PA
CBHW070738230426
43669CB00014B/2496